The Art of Whisky

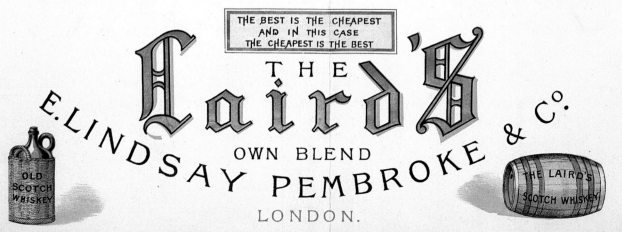

THE ART OF
WHISKY

A De Luxe Blend of Historic Posters
from the Public Record Office

JIM MURRAY

PRO PUBLICATIONS

DEDICATION

To my great and dear friend, the cartoonist Bill Caldwell who gave me such enormous support and encouragement when I needed it most during my earliest whisky writing days. Thank you.

ACKNOWLEDGEMENTS

First and foremost I must say thank you to all those at the Public Record Office, Kew, for their unwavering help and efficiency, especially Paul Sinnott who spent much so much time wading through boxes of ancient treasures; Brian Carter who photographed all the original posters; and my editor Julia Wigg for kindly involving me in this wonderful project and then providing all further information I needed with patience, charm and good humour. From the whisky industry I would like to thank a quartet of highly experienced and knowledgeable blenders, Richard Paterson, Ian Grieve, Jim Milne and David Stewart for offering advice and suggestions when my own researches and records had drawn a blank. Also thanks go to Charles Craig on his achievement of compiling the incomparable and indispensable *Scotch Whisky Industry Record* which made some sense of the drawerfuls of documents in my possession, to Makie Ando and my daughter Tabitha for helping when time was so tight, and finally to my boys James and David for putting up with my being locked in my office for days on end.

PRO Publications
Public Record Office
Ruskin Avenue
Kew, Surrey
TW9 4DU

ISBN 1 873162 67 7

Book design by Roger Hammond
Production consultant Geoff Barlow
Printed in Italy by Grafiche Milani S.p.A.

A catalogue card for this book is available from the British Library

FRONTISPIECE:
A splendidly romantic vision of the aged highlander enjoying his whisky advertises the Laird's Own Blend in 1888.
COPY 1/81 f 367

CONTENTS

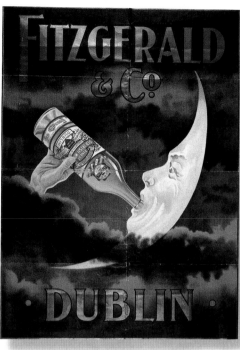

BROWN'S
Special
SCOTCH WHISKY

Used in the
PALACE

AND

SHIEL

TRADE  MARK

J. Brown & Co. LONDON & GLASGOW.

BROWN'S STORES AND BRANCHES,
STOKE NEWINGTON.

PREFACE

There is no doubt that the making of whisky is an art, as is blending whisky: it is all too easy to make bad single malts and blends. However, among the plethora of books on whisky that has hit the shelves of late there is an art form that has been sadly overlooked. It is found in the posters used to advertise the rising star of the world's spirits, as whisky was in that eventful period at the close of the Victorian age and the opening of the Edwardian.

Whisky advertising exists in numerous forms: labels, post-cards, newspaper advertise-ments, pub mirrors. But it was the splendid range of posters which caught my eye long ago to become my favourite. Not those appallingly crass smoothie ads of the 1960s and 1970s which concentrated on making whisky the key to an executive lifestyle full of expensive suits and teeth-filled smiles: the period I found irre-sistible was the romantic one when Britain still had an empire, servants knew their

A pretty Scotch lassie advertises Tartan Blend in 1898.
COPY 1/140 f 284

Opposite: Brown's Special Scotch Whisky was meant to appeal equally to all, whatever their position in society.
COPY 1/119 f 222

permanent grin. It was a time when tastelessness had been perfected to become an art form in itself.

But not all whisky advertis-ing was quite so naïve. Some companies took great delight in showing whisky's place in the Empire. And there was often a peg on which to hang humour, nationalistic pride or classical elegance. It was then that some of the best artwork was commissioned.

This is one of four whisky books I will have written dur-ing 1998. Yet, if truth be told, it was the one I was looking forward most to write, partly because this is a novel way to tell the early history of whisky in bite-sized chunks, but not least to gain some insight into so many brands now sadly missed. The Public Record Office at Kew kindly asked if I would like to write a book based on the posters for whisky which form a small part of the archive of copy-right designs registered between 1862 and 1912, orig-inally held at Stationers' Hall

place and anyone with a modicum of good taste could instantly recognise a fine whisky, but only with a splash of soda.

This was also an era long before the advent of Political Correctness. So chaps from overseas were appallingly patronised, stereotypes abounded and no self-respecting Scotsman would be drawn without a kilt, (on postcards a tightly bound purse) and a Fraseresque look on his usually orange-bearded face that told us: 'We're doomed!' By startling contrast, his Irish counter-part jigged about in a silly hat, green jacket and

in London and later transferred to the PRO. The bulk of the material dates from about 1885 onwards, and regis-tration was always entirely voluntary, so the PRO's files are far from complete. But what we unearthed during the researching of this book reveals a compelling cross-sec-tion of a charming art form, but one so antediluvian as to have been buried almost without trace.

JIM MURRAY,
Wellingborough, February 1998

AN HISTORICAL PORTRAIT

THERE ARE ANY number of misconceptions when it comes to whisky. And perhaps the greatest of them all is about the 'good old days'. Read the marketing blurb on late twentieth-century posters and magazine advertisements, not to mention the back of labels or on the boxes and canisters which package the bottles, and more than occasionally you will discover copy-writers of post-war brands waxing lyrical about yesteryear and how a whisky today will taste just as it did a hundred years ago.

My hope is that it in most cases it won't. Because, contrary to popular myth, Scotch whisky – malt and blended, provided the 'whisky' was made in a distillery at all – was not produced to quite the same high specifications as today. That is not to say that it was all bad. It is just that Scotch and Irish, like Bourbon and even Canadian, is now distilled and matured with greater care and precision than when the industry was still in its relative infancy.

Indeed, it was because there were so many poor whiskies around during late Victorian and early Edwardian times that distillers of that era went to such great lengths to promote theirs as a superior product. A number, it has to be said, were stretching the truth. Others, including the vast majority of brands included in this book, would have been very drinkable, while there were genuinely high quality whiskies to the extent that brands like Teacher's, Dewar's and Buchanan's have survived to this day and are still rightly celebrated as top performance drams. And although I can vouch that their whisky was excellent – I have even been lucky enough to taste some better-known blends from that romantic period – it is unlikely that they would have achieved commercial prominence on quality alone. Advertising played a vital role in bringing these products to the public's attention, some of it subtly by using recommendations from high-ranking officials to hit a small but opinion-forming clientele, and then more generally through striking artwork which caught the eye of

Some blenders, and Dewar's in particular, liked to use classic artistic values to demonstrate the quality of their whisky. To complete a set of portraits of *The Laird*, *The Connoisseur* and *The Squire* came this one, *The Dandy*, proving that whisky appealed to the practised palate ninety years ago just as today.
COPY 1/310 f 187.

either the masses or those of a comfortable social class.

As we shall see through these posters, advertising moved a long way from the earlier pay-by-the-word lineage taken out in the local and then national press, such as James Buchanan's uncharacteristically self-effacing notice of 1884 which simply read: 'The "Buchanan Blend" of Fine Old Scotch Whiskies Suitable either for Grog or Toddy.' Soon distillers and blenders were looking for themes which could be immediately and consistently identified with their own brands.

And as the nineteenth century progressed so, too, did the confidence of the blenders. Communications within Britain were improving almost monthly with an ever growing rail network that meant whisky could be supplied in no time at all to any part of the country. Not that the expansion of the industry was confined within these shores: Britain was now the centre of an empire that criss-crossed the world and expatriates in burgeoning new economies such as those of South Africa, Australia, New Zealand and Rhodesia needed to be supplied with the creature comforts of home. And that included whisky.

The quarter of a century covered by this book was perhaps the most turbulent and in many ways most fascinating in the history of the Scotch and Irish whisky industries. It was a period that experienced a crescendo of activity following the mounting popularity of a drink that had seen boom and bust like none other before. In the powerful whisky barons and a posse of smaller-scale honest aspirants it had spawned a whole new breed of entrepreneur, as well as any number of unscrupulous sharks who were desperate to make a killing from a nation's, if not a world's, newly-found love.

There was nothing new about whisky attracting lawbreakers. Before it ever became a mass-marketed and respectable drink, there had been *uisge-beatha*, Gaelic for 'the water of life', and it had come in a pure, traditional form, distilled in oversized kettles known as copper pot stills, with the use of cold running water from a spring found in some lonely highland glen or Irish field. In the highlands and islands of Scotland the distillers would use nothing but barley which they would malt themselves; in Ireland (as later became the occasional mode in lowland Scotland) the practice often included the use of unmalted barley or even oats which gave it a lighter, fruitier character. Few of these distilleries were legal, in fact only a handful of early distillers bothered to pay the British Government for a licence, and those who did were often despised by their neighbours for so doing. The markets this illicit produce found would be in nearby towns and cities, the spirit smuggled behind the backs of the pistol-packing Custom and Excise officers to a thirsty and appreciative populace.

But during the eighteenth century and the first part of the nineteenth, in the grand scheme of British social life this whisky was little more than a parochial pleasantry; a curiosity to the likes of Dr Samuel Johnson who was one of the few not entirely to dismiss the native spirit of those remote and rugged lands as something too uncouth for gentlemen and probably for the civilised world as a whole. To those who made it, it was something very much more: a liquid form of national identity and vital to the economy of the small farmer who found that he could make more from his grain when distilled than when sold as a crop. On top of that it tasted rather good, too.

This poster from September 1898 is a fine example of how whisky companies sprang up in London to serve the Empire and beyond.
COPY 1/143ii f 1.

The common view of whisky's questionable pedigree was set to change. And as Britain instigated the world's industrial revolution, whisky was to be caught up in the turning cogs of transition clanking through the nation, and as a result propelled from relative obscurity into the public domain with such force and speed that soon no self-respecting public house would be found without a bottle or even a cask.

What had always been problems regarding the making of whisky were the cost and the taste of the resulting product. Pot stills were inefficient vessels which needed much fuel for heating and time and labour for cleaning out after every use. Also, the size of the still led to a heavy whisky full of the flavours of the barley and the peat used in the kilning of the malt. The smaller the still, the oilier and more full-bodied the spirit tended to be, with the copper having a big say in the style of the spirit. Then there was the art of the stillman, the person responsible for deciding which spirit was potable and which was to be re-distilled. When pure malt whisky is made, the spirit which runs off the second (or sometimes third) still is split into the heads, middle and tails. The heads and tails are full of undesirable elements needing re-distillation. It is the middle, the heart of the run, which is selected for barrelling and maturation. Too often, to save money distillers did not bother very much about the details of these fractions, so spirit in dire need of re-distillation ended up in the barrel. And because illicit distillers generally used small stills that could be easily carried, in their case it was doubtful if the whisky went through any second distillation at all. Whatever they made they would sell.

What some commercial distillers began to strive for was a method of making whisky not by the traditional, tried and tested but cumbersome batch pot still procedure but by a continuous means to save time, labour and money. The race was on all over the world. As well as Scotch and Irish distillers looking into the problem so were distillers in France and Germany and in the USA where a new type of whiskey known as Bourbon had by then become enormously popular. It is likely that the first continuous stills were tried and tested in America but with mixed results. Robert Stein got his continuous still going during the 1820s but it was not until 1830 that the system was perfected by Aeneas Coffey, a British Government employee, who was officially head of Customs and Excise for Ireland and unofficially an inventor who in many ways was responsible for the success of whisky today.

In Britain these continuous stills, called patent stills after the copyright patents Coffey and Stein took out on them, at first sometimes ran using expensive malted barley, but as costs were shaved further it was decided to use higher proportions of unmalted barley. That remained the case until 1846 when the repeal of the Corn Laws meant distillers could buy other, cheaper grains, notably maize. This suited distillers on two counts. Not only was it cheaper to buy, but the alcohol yield from this North American corn was actually higher. Curiously, 150 years on the practice of making malt through continuous stills has not entirely died out. They still do so at Kasauli Distillery in the Himalayas, built originally to serve British soldiers in India.

A pleasing and fortuitous side effect of continuous distillation for these distillers was the fact that the whisky was distilled to a higher proof and was therefore cleaner and lighter in character. One of the reasons pot still Scotch had never taken England by storm was because it was regarded as too powerful and uncompromising in taste. The smokiness of the peat which had been used in the malting clung limpet-like to the glass and the tastebuds. And sometimes there was an oiliness which seemed as dark, strange and mysterious as the country from which it had come. Instead, most drinkers preferred brandy, a much lighter spirit squeezed from the grape rather than grain. However, in the 1880s disaster was to hit the French wine and cognac industry. The *phylloxera vastatrix* had begun to decimate vines throughout the country and British importers had to look elsewhere for regular supplies of spirit. First it was the lighter Irish whiskies, which had already begun to seep into the spirit market, that were preferred. Then Scotch began to take control.

This was because, unlike the Irish, Scotch whisky merchants were prepared to mix single malt whisky with the lighter grain in order to soften the flavour. This blended whisky, or mixture as it was initially known, took some time to evolve. It was in 1860 that the Spirits Act allowed the blending together of malt and grain whisky, a practice that had until

Above: Sport and humour were often used in Edwardian whisky posters and here they are combined to ingenious effect.
COPY 1/298 f 263

Left: The Old Orkney Distillery made good use of a mild joke in this showcard of 1904.
COPY 1/219i f 69

then been against the law. Blending was first commercially pursued by Andrew Usher and possibly Charles Mackinlay soon after but it was not until 1865 with the emergence of Usher's Old Vatted Glenlivet that this new whisky style became available to the public. It soon became all the rage. Throughout Scotland merchants began buying in supplies of malt and grain whiskies and blending them together. All over the country whisky blending companies began to flourish, though usually with not quite the same success as their rivals north of the border. Such were the houses of Bells, Sandeman of VAT 69 fame, Dewar's, Buchanan and others, built sometimes slowly, occasionally with spectacular swiftness of success.

Curiously, at that time blenders were delighted if people remarked on how lacking in strong flavours their blend was. Where today every self-respecting whisky has accompanying tasting notes – some on the button, others just wishful thinking – in those days blenders were quite delighted if their creations were regarded as 'bland'. For instance take this extract from the October 1905 edition of the *War Office Times* and *Naval Review* which wrote of the VAT 69 blend: 'This grand whisky has been a revelation to us, the whisky is bland and smooth to the taste...' This was by no means a criticism. On the contrary: they were heaping lavish praise upon it. Yet very few advertisements ever actually discussed the nature of the beast in the bottle. What they sometimes made a point of underlining was the purity of their whisky. A common phrase used by more than one blender (see page 18) was 'not a headache in a bottle'.

There was certainly justification for trying to win customers over on that point. At the end of the nineteenth century the quality of whisky which people were being served was becoming too horrible to contemplate, let alone drink. On both sides of the Atlantic another more sinister art form was being perfected: that of making so-called whisky from compounds which had never been within a hundred miles of an authentic still. So serious did this problem become that between the 1870s and 1890s there was widespread outrage at this adulteration in which turpentine, methylated spirits and even sulphuric acid were often components. Analysts the length and breath of Britain, it seemed, were trying to discover just what these bogus whiskies contained. It was another decade, though, before a Royal Commission sat to ponder another question which was vexing distiller, blender and consumer alike: what is whisky?

The distillers of traditional pot still malt spirit felt that they were the only people with a right to call their products whisky. While the poisonous adulteration of whisky was carried out by an entirely different and sinister breed of merchant, pot still producers did not have very much time for the distillers of continuous still malt spirits either.

In Ireland, Dublin's four most prominent distillers, John Jameson, William Jameson, John Power and George Roe in 1878 even went so far as to produce their own beautifully illustrated book, *Truths About Whisky*, demanding that grain whiskey should be banned from being sold as whiskey and stating that the only true Irish whiskey was the rich fruit of the copper pot. They were first peeved by the fact that merchants had begun blending their pot still whiskies with what they regarded as inferior country pot still and selling it off as top

Another sporting poster with a gentle play on words, always so beloved of the Edwardian copy-writer.
COPY 1/224 f 206

grade Dublin whiskey. But their anger at that practice was nothing compared to their reaction to another scam: 'Pressure was next brought to bear upon the revenue authorities to permit 'Blending' of 'Plain British Spirit' in bond; and dealers were allowed to bring silent spirit [spirit distilled by continuous rather than batch-pot method] from any part of the United Kingdom to any other part, and to mix it with any other spirit, being of British manufacture, in any proportions which seemed good to them. Great manufactories of silent spirit existed in Scotland; but Irish whiskey was held in more general esteem than Scotch, and so the Scotch and English silent spirit was sent to Dublin to be returned from thence to England as Dublin or Irish Whisky. Thousands of gallons of silent spirit were sent from Glasgow or from Liverpool to Dublin or to Belfast; and having been mixed in bond with other spirit like itself, from the same or from other sources, and perhaps with a little, say, 10 per cent., of genuine coarse Whisky, the compound was reshipped immediately from the Irish port, with a Belfast or Dublin Custom-House permit, as Dublin or Irish Whisky and was sold under that name in England, and was sent from England to all other parts of the world.'

This might at first sight be dismissed as protectionist scare-mongering. But this account was not only accurate in its revealing of how the world's Irish whisky drinkers were being duped, but they were quite right about Irish being the preferred whisky. In 1875 a fraction over two out of every three bottles of whisky sold by the London-based whisky merchants W A Gilbey was Irish as opposed to Scotch. But at least Gilbey whiskey remained entirely unadulterated: being close to the Dublin distillers, John Jameson in particular, they had also been swayed on the question of blend or not to blend.

Meanwhile, the move towards mixing patent still spirit with pot still gathered pace and a great many firms did so without resorting to chemical adulteration. The British market had showed that it preferred its whisky light. Still the upper classes had to be won over: whisky had always been regarded as a working-class tipple. But through the enormous combined energies of James Buchanan, Tommy Dewar, the slightly eccentric Peter Mackie of White Horse fame and others, the wheel of opinion began to change, as can be seen through the style of many of the posters to be found in this book.

But the malt whisky distillers had not yet had their day. They saw the patent whisky distillers not only as a threat to their existence but to the industry's as a whole. There was mixed logic behind their resentment. Certainly the amount of malt whisky found in some blends could be counted in mere fractions; on the other hand the British public outside the Scottish highlands had already shown that they did not much care for this very strongly flavoured spirit from north of the border.

The battle came to a head in 1909 when Islington Council took action against a couple of local off-licensees for selling whisky which was not up to the standard they had claimed. Magistrates sided with the council and the shock waves rumbled through the giant Distillers Company Limited, which had first formed in the 1850s when a group of grain distillers teamed together to strengthen their new line of business and had since been on an upward curve of expansion. Firing a volley in return, DCL then promoted the pure grain whisky from Cambus distillery as Scotch, as the Government at last set up a commission to determine once and for all what constituted whisky. To the horror of the malt distillers and a number of independent whisky experts of the time, notably JA Nettleton, they found in favour of the grain distillers.

Yet without doubt their decision was the saviour of many of Scotland's malt whisky distilleries still in operation today, because even now, during the present increase in the popularity of malt, nine out of every ten bottles bought are blended. Malt whisky distilleries were usually run by small companies and families; a few were owned by blenders, either to guarantee stocks of malt at prices they could control or simply just because it sounded more commercially significant to be dubbed 'Distillers and Blenders'

During the 1890s and 1900s government Select Committees and special boards sat almost every year to debate aspects of the whisky trade. Here Bushmills have cleverly turned a sitting to their advantage.
COPY 1/138ii f 153.

as opposed to blenders alone. Independent highland distillers, though, tended not to be financially sound and many distilleries have, over the years, fallen into receivership.

Just how thin was that line between success and failure had been amply demonstrated in 1898 when one of Scotland's most enigmatic (to some, dubious to others) whisky companies, Pattison, crashed. Despite all the unscrupulous practices which abounded, it seemed everyone wanted to invest in Scotch whisky. A succession of distilleries were built in the highlands of Scotland. In the 1870s and 1880s they had been built where the stronger flavoured whiskies were traditionally found: Islay, Campbeltown and the remoter highland areas. In the 1890s it was Speyside's turn to be littered with building sites as one distillery after another was erected to bask in the reflected fame of the Glenlivet name. The Glenlivet distillery was located to the west of the region in one of the remotest glens and its whisky was regarded as the finest Scotland had to offer. So distilleries built nowhere near the River Livet made a point of

Whisky was perceived as a man's world in 1912 and every example of art in this book was drawn by men – with the exception of this curious effort by Jessie Bolingbroke Price. It is hard to imagine that as powerful a distiller as Haig & Haig ever put it to use.
COPY 1/316 f 334.

making Glenlivet part of their name, which they were legally entitled to do providing they added a dash before they did so.

As this move to get into whisky became a stampede, two brothers from a Leith grocer's and wine merchant's firm, Robert and Walter Pattison, began to deal more aggressively than most. Being based in Leith and having the very good sense to supply tied houses, always a guarantee of sales, their credentials appeared impressive. At one stage the company seemed to be a match for Dewar's, Teacher's and others. But where those famous concerns handled their money with caution and used profits to re-invest for consolidation and expansion of the business, the Pattison brothers used money coming in, including proceeds from a flotation, for building themselves luxurious houses, furnishing palatial offices and living the most sumptuous of lifestyles. Banks were lending heavily to a number of companies, Pattisons included, as demand for whisky appeared to show no sign of abating. But in reality there was far more whisky being produced than could ever be sold, especially now there were more and more distilleries in production and more merchants making orders for sales which were only there on paper in two, three or four years' time. Eventually it became apparent that Pattisons were trading fraudulently and when their inevitable crash came, leading at length to the imprisonment of both brothers, confidence in the industry evaporated. Pattisons' whisky stocks accounted for less than a fifth of one per cent of all that existing in the industry, but with traders already jittery, nerve gave way and the exodus from the industry was alarming. The value of whisky, for a long time over-inflated, dipped, as did the worth of companies and banks pulled out. In some ways it all played into the hands of companies such as DCL who were large enough to absorb such shock-waves; indeed they found themselves able to buy whisky stocks and companies at much lower prices.

As the strength of DCL continued, blenders such as Teacher's, Dewar's, Buchanan and Johnnie Walker worked tirelessly to become financially strong enough to withstand any hostile advance from a clearly predatory company. Meanwhile

Above: This poster from February 1898 depicts a ship bound for disaster. Only ten months later the company ran aground and sank without trace, with the Pattison brothers jailed for fraud and embezzlement. The ripples from the sinking ship caused panic throughout the industry and ended the boom years of distillery building and speculation.
COPY 1/138ii f 68.

Left: If any poster summarised the failure of Pattisons, this is it. In its short life the company traded too quickly into too wide a market, and spent enormous sums on employing salesmen and on the commissioning of advertising such as this to support them. This really was the final toast – only a few months later the company crashed spectacularly.
COPY 1/143ii f 303.

smaller firms tried to emulate these successful blenders by finding markets the world over for a spirit which had now been accepted across the social spectrum as being a dram fit for a king.

It is against this busy and turbulent background that we now take a look at the posters...

THE POSTERS

THORNE'S WHISKY

This delightful vision depicting 'Scotland's Pride' offers something of a paradox. At first glance we see a symbol of purity: the freshly picked barley as it is before being turned to malt and the horned drinking vessel suggesting a noble timelessness beyond the bar-room tumbler. But there is also a hint of temptation, first with the subtle revealing of the shoulder and bosom and then the more flagrant discarding of the shoe, exposing dangerous red stockings.

Maybe this stunning drawing, resorting only to a tasteful tartan as a geographical stereotype, is nothing more than a pun: a Scottish rose beside a Thorne. Either way, it perfectly reflects the beauty and danger of drinking Scotch.

The whisky in question is only a little less intriguing. R. Thorne & Sons were founded in 1831 and when this poster was lodged at Stationers' Hall, they were reaching the zenith of their powers. By then they were not only blenders but themselves distillers, owning the now defunct Greenock Lowland distillery, in their home town, and the now famous Aberlour Distillery in Speyside. Just a year earlier, in 1897, they had played the lead role in converting Glen Moray from a brewery into a distillery. Despite such apparent strength, the company failed in 1920 and bears no relation to the Thomas Thorne whisky brand owned by Allied Domecq. However, on their demise R. Thorne and Son sold Aberlour to Holts of Chorlton cum Hardy who held on to it until 1945. Then it was snapped up by Campbell Distillers which, as a subsidiary of Pernod Ricard, owns it to this day. Glen Moray also lives on as one of three distilleries owned by Glenmorangie.

Artist: W. H Waller
Date of registration: 24 November 1898
PRO reference: COPY 1/144ii f 76

JAMES BUCHANAN & CO. SPECIAL SCOTCH WHISKY

James Buchanan was not a man to do things by halves. For a young Canadian-born Scot who began life in the whisky industry as a salesman for Charles Mackinlay, he progressed with almost ruthless determination, becoming one of the great whisky barons of the late Victorian period.

He enjoyed all the social trappings along the way (indeed, he was later to become Lord Woolavington) and this is underlined by the tone of this poster. The royal warrants of Her Majesty Queen Victoria and HRH The Prince of Wales take pride of place at the head of the design. But on the label itself it is the House of Commons, printed in deep red, which catches the eye. Buchanan, in his quest to keep ahead of his rivals, cleverly used a letter from the Refreshments Committee on headed Commons writing paper showing their desire to buy his Scotch. Likewise, in Ireland the Coleraine distillery exploited their famous 'H.C.' trademark, having had their malt in the Commons since 1843.

Buchanan's whisky, however, was a blend. The very first label was less proud, suggesting his whisky should be used for 'Grog or Toddy'. The label following the one depicted here was slightly modified to be called 'Red Seal'. However, once the House of Commons link had served its purpose all titles were dropped at the turn of the century in favour of the popular nickname bestowed on it by the public: 'Black and White', on account of the white label on the black bottle. The brand thrives to this day, though mainly in export markets.

Artist: Robert Casey
Date of registration: 29 September 1899
PRO reference: COPY 1/146ii f 29

PER **3/6** BOTTLE

"Old Reading Abbey"
Scotch & Irish
Whisky

Thoroughly Matured & of Guaranteed Age.

REGISTERED TRADE MARK

Sole Proprietors
Butler & Sons, Reading.

BEMROSE, LIMITED, DERBY.

COPYRIGHT

FRIAR ROYD FINE OLD SCOTCH WHISKY

OLD READING ABBEY SCOTCH AND IRISH WHISKY

No matter how saintly monks were considered to be, or how Spartan their worldly lives, the one thing they were considered to excel in was drinking and eating. Throughout European literature and mythology the monk was perceived as a venerable glutton.

For this reason all over Europe monks can be found in advertising posters imbibing wine, spirits, liqueurs and beer and usually with contented faces and paunches to match. The fact they often made these beverages for themselves was one reason the jolly monk was seen as a useful means by which the artist could illustrate the themes of high quality and long tradition.

In the case of Scotch whisky there was double good cause. The very first record of Scotch being made is found in the Scottish Exchequer Rolls for 1494: 'Eight bolls of malt to Friar John Cor, by order of the King, wherewith to make aqua vitae.' Now it could have been that Friar John was making his *aqua vitae* – whisky – for medicinal reasons, as distillation was often used for the making of medicines. But in the two posters here the point of drinking whisky is undoubtedly for the pleasure of consumption.

Both posters were made for non-distillers who would have bought whisky from various sources and blended them together, probably for local trade. For 'Old Reading Abbey' a cost-cutting exercise has been taken in advertising both their Scotch and Irish brands in one poster. The idea is that the drinking of whisky was every bit as natural as being given their daily bread. In the poster for Holroyd's whisky the monks have eschewed any accompanying food to concentrate on the Scotch. The 'Friar Royd' poster of 1898, in the typically lush style of Arthur Clark pre-dates 'Old Reading Abbey' by seven years. Both brands, however, have long since met their makers.

Friar Royd

Artist: Arthur Clark

Date of registration: 19 January 1898

PRO reference: COPY 1/138ii f 131

Old Reading Abbey:

Artist: Peter Campbell

Date of registration: 10 May 1905

PRO reference: COPY 1/229i f 159

GLENCUPAR

It was one of the most common themes of its age: 'not a headache in a dram'; 'not a headache in a bottle', 'not a headache in a barrel'. All these terms, and more, can be found in whisky advertising posters during the first decade of the twentieth century. And all are tied in with the big 'What is Whisky?' debate raging at the time. It was the claim of blenders, and not without some scientific proof, that the use of grain whiskies lightens the dram and lessens the chance or intensity of headaches from drinking too much of it.

This 1909 version, 'A Case of No Headaches' from a minor whisky company is perhaps the neatest joke on the theme. The dozen heads corking the bottles are possibly luminaries of the era: they look too distinctive to be just ordinary faces in the crowd. And what Napoleon, found in the back row, would have thought of being used to push the sales of whisky rather than cognac is anybody's guess.

The name of Andrew Reid found in the bottom left hand corner has no connection with the famous founder of the Macallan Distillery. Reid was the Newcastle-based printing firm local to the Gateshead Wine and Spirit Company and was known for its fine quality of reproduction for a number of Scottish-based whisky companies, including Daniel Crawford & Son.

Artist: Fred Simpson
Date of registration: 9 July 1909
PRO Reference: COPY 1/ 283 f 302

BUSHMILLS

This curious poster shows the unmistakable label of Bushmills, one of only three distilleries operating in Ireland today and the last in Ulster. The lack of any slick copy could mean that the artist had the dual role of providing both a poster and postcard. Either way, the actual meaning of the two men and the hidden bottle is not particularly easy to fathom, especially as the bottles on the bar are also obviously Bushmills.

In what is now Northern Ireland, distillers tended to spell their make 'whisky' without an 'e'. Bushmills had been an exception to the rule. The bottle also clearly states Pure Malt, for which the distillery is still famed today. But it was not until around 1891 that they produced that form of whiskey. Before that, they had made 'Pot Still' whiskey, a style peculiar to the Irish where unmalted barley was mixed with malted barley. It had also been practised in the Lowlands of Scotland many years before but

died out probably in the early to mid nineteenth century.

Today's Bushmills, with a white label strikingly similar to that of ninety years ago, is a blended whiskey. This label clearly shows the date of the distillery's establishment, 1784. This proud information was also moulded onto the bottle for good measure.

Artist: Henry Brewerton Quinan
Date of registration: 11 December 1907
PRO reference: COPY 1/264 f 237

LEITH'S SPECIAL

At the tail end of the twentieth century it has become all the rage in the USA to don evening dress and taste whisky with cigar in hand. It appears, though, that those attending these smoky evenings are a century behind the times.

This simple but effective poster by the Aberdeen wine merchants James Leith wallows in understated luxury. The cigar, the garb, the leather chair and even the servant's bell leave one in little doubt that this is a man of good taste and wealth. So what does he drink? Leith's whisky, naturally. And the punchline, ' So, Here's Luck!' appears to encompass more than the whisky alone, as the broad wink testifies.

James Leith was one of many whisky merchants found in the Granite City during that era. Aberdeen enjoyed the dual benefit of being close to Speyside and a port, and at that time even had its own distillery, the Bon Accord, which was destroyed by fire in 1885. After being rebuilt it failed in the year of this poster. With Bon Accord in such dire need of money, it would be reasonable to assume that some of its whisky found its way into 'Leith's Special'.

Artist: William Robertson Smith
Date of registration: 31 December 1906
PRO reference: COPY 1/253 f 417

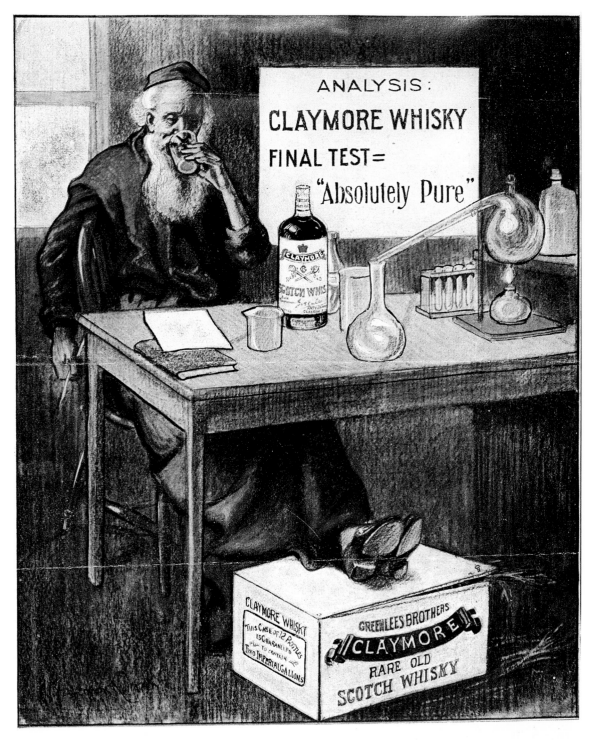

ANALYSIS:
CLAYMORE WHISKY
FINAL TEST =
"Absolutely Pure"

CLAYMORE WHISKY

SCOTCH WHISKY

CLAYMORE WHISKY
THIS CASE OF 12 BOTTLES
IS GUARANTEED
TO CONTAIN
TWO IMPERIAL GALLONS

GREENLEES BROTHERS
CLAYMORE
RARE OLD
SCOTCH WHISKY

COPYRIGHT.   ENTERED AT STATIONERS' HALL

"TIRED NATURE'S SWEET RESTORER."

CLAYMORE WHISKY

Distillers and blenders went to great lengths to show that their whisky was of unquestionable quality. And an analyst's certificate was one popular way to relieve a potential customer from any fears that he was buying an adulterated product.

To this end, Greenlees Brothers, at that time one of the most famous names in distilling, went a step further and even had a little fun at the expense of the analyst himself. The one depicted here appears to be studying their Claymore blend in perhaps even greater detail than his call of duty demands. And one can safely assume from his relaxed manner that there is no reason to doubt the contents of the bottle.

Greenlees Brothers were for a long time connected to the Glendullan Distillery in Speyside which in turn, with the Claymore brand, became part of the Distillers Company Limited, now United Distillers and Vintners. The Claymore, as it is now known, remains one of Britain's best-selling brands, but is today owned by Whyte and Mackay, a subsidiary of Jim Beam Brands.

Artist: Henry Brewerton Quinan
Date of registration: 11 December 1907
PRO reference: COPY 1/264 f 189

O.O. IS NEEDED IN LONDON

During the first decade of the twentieth century it was still rare to find single malt whisky being advertised in England. But there were one or two exceptions and Old Orkney was one of the boldest of its era. Of course, stating that 'O.O.' is needed in London is more of a pun on the letters rather than a statement of fact. Sadly, it did not seem to be needed much anywhere: the Stromness Distillery where O.O. was made closed down in 1928 never to re-open.

O.O. whisky posters made a point of showing a Scotsman in full regalia. This may be linked with why, very unusually, this pure malt was called 'Pot Still' whisky, a mainly Irish term. Not only was the advertising agency and artist from Belfast, but so were the distillery's owners, McConnell's. With non-Scotsmen responsible for the advertising, it is no surprise that they resorted to national stereotypes.

However, it appears that artist Frank Riley may have been having a dram or two over the top as he sought inspiration: on the bottle held in the right arm of the clansman the Stromness Distillery has been re-dubbed Stormness. Or maybe he was simply alluding to some typically bracing weather he had encountered on that windy isle. It certainly seems, though, that he had never been to London. The turreted skyline is distinctly Scottish.

Artist: Frank Riley
Date of registration: 29 October 1906
PRO reference: COPY 1/250 f 328

BEATSON, MCLEOD & CO. LTD

Here is a charming poster that has it all: romance, a reference to Glenlivet and a pun. The artist appears to have been allowed free rein to his skills. The glass contains not whisky as such, but a toddy: a mixture of whisky, hot water and sugar – hence the glass stirrer to mix the draught which would be taken on cold winter evenings to warm the body and lift the spirits. It was also a favourite for medicinal purposes and is still used as such today.

The marvellous apparition which wafts from the glass is reminiscent of a genie let loose but more striking as the spirit of Scotch whose Celtic blue eyes are both hypnotic and haunting. Of the two bottles it is Culdees Glenlivet which is given centre stage. There was no distillery by the name of Culdee: it refers to a member of an ancient Scots-Irish religious order and was originally a name given to a recluse. The Glenlivet title was used simply as a way of impressing customers. Certainly it would not be 100% whisky from The Glenlivet distillery and may contain none at all.

The pun is in the name: 'Beats One and All' comes from Beatson and McLeod, probably established by David Beatson of Kirkcaldy, one of the founding shareholders of the North British grain whisky distillery still operating in Edinburgh today.

Artist: Sydney Smith
Date of registration: 1 April 1903
PRO reference: COPY 1/202ii f 81

'BANTASKIN' AND 'OLD SILENT' MALT LIQUEUR HIGHLAND WHISKIES

A fellow minor shareholder in the North British distillery (a modest 50 as compared to the 400 held by notables such as Andrew Usher) was Benjamin Mackay of Lenzie. His was another whisky merchant whose star shone dimly and relatively briefly at the turn of the century.

The fact that he was ambitious enough to invest in a stake of a grain whisky distillery reveals that he was among those who saw their fortune being made on the back of blended rather than pure malt whisky, and that his plans did not simply cover the short term.

Sadly, both his 'Bantaskin' and 'Old Silent' brands have long since disappeared but this poster from 1902, despite its apparent laird, ghillie and piper cliché, offers an not entirely unrealistic look at social life in the Highlands where thatch was once a common roofing material. Perhaps one discordant note is the odd choice of promoting 'Old Silent' whisky with an advertisement featuring the wailing of the bagpipe.

Artist: William McCallum
Date of registration: 17 October 1902
PRO reference: COPY 1/195i f 159

DANIEL CRAWFORD & SON

Look closely at the Scottish dancers and piper. Do they look familiar? They should. These, quite amazingly, are the same characters found celebrating Mackay's whiskies. Except there is something just a little different about them. Most seem a little younger. Reeling about without his swords, the dancer on the left has retained the last flush of youth; the ghillie's sideburns are nothing like so lush or his face so full; the dancer

centre stage appears to be sitting it out with a bottle of Mackay on the table before him, defeated by age. Only the piper, tapping out his familiar beat, seems to have confounded old Father Time.

There is a simple explanation for all this. Despite the two posters promoting two entirely unconnected whiskies, the artist used for them was the same: William McCallum of Glasgow. When commissioned for the Mackay whisky in 1902 he obviously decided to go back to his old friends which he created for

this poster in 1896. And because six years had passed he whimsically aged them accordingly. It also appears that the dancers had caught the spirit of the age: in 1896 they were drinking malt whisky. Six years later they were drinking a blend. Pay the artist his fee and they might have been drinking Irish.

Artist: William McCallum
Date of registration: 10 November 1896
PRO reference: COPY 1/130 ii f 138

THE BEST PEG

One of the most popular markets Scotch blenders tried to conquer was among the soldiers and officers posted to distant lands to protect Britain's Empire. And of those, India was seen by some as a golden nugget.

That may explain this outwardly bizarre advertisement from the Glasgow blenders Daniel Crawford and Son. What we see here is a Bengal Lancer 'Tent Pegging', an exhibition in the craft of horsemanship and lancing. It also appears to have been the peg (which is also a drinking vessel) on which to hang a rather weak pun for Daniel Crawford's FVO Scotch Whisky. As we know, FVO stands for Finest Very Old, though now there is no mention of it just being a malt as was the case 16 years earlier.

This poster was also a final hurrah for Daniel Crawford and Son. The fact it was accepted as a suitable advertisement for the whisky perhaps revealed something of the state of mind of the 'Son', Eunig Crawford. Exactly a year after this poster was lodged at the Stationers' Hall, he retired from the industry and sold the business to the Distillers Company Limited.

Artist: Arthur Gough
Date of registration: 9 March 1912
PRO reference: COPY 1/316 f 232

I ALWAYS TAKE

For collectors, it is always the flawed specimen which has extra rarity value. So what price this poster lodged with the Stationers' Hall in January 1907?

It certainly shows how some advertising agencies worked, in this case George Harrison and Sons of Bradford. Someone there has a good wheeze: in this case a burglar breaking into a house, ignoring the family silver and focusing on the bottle of whisky. The working caption would be 'I always take... ' Now what needed filling in was the name of the whisky.

It appears, ironically, that there were no takers and for ninety years the poster has remained in the files of first the Stationers' Hall and then the Public Record Office waiting for the label to be filled in...

Artist: Arthur Helsby
Date of registration: 18 January 1907
PRO reference: COPY 1/253 f 200

ROBERTSON'S YELLOW LABEL

You might get the feeling that this advertisement for Robertson's Yellow Label Special Scotch perhaps came about in the same way as 'I Always Take'. The idyllic English country scene looks better suited to a good old-fashioned country ale than a spirit. But the catch lines of 'The Travellers Joy' and 'Worth Hunting For' were obviously an irresistible temptation.

This brand, today registered with United Distillers and Vintners, can still be found in Spain and, if you keep your eyes peeled, very occasionally in the UK. But the distillery owned by John Robertson and Sons at the time of this poster, Coleburn near Elgin, finally closed in 1984. Coleburn whisky, never one of the finest to be made on Speyside, would certainly have been used in the blending of the brand depicted here.

As recently as 1992, some Scottish tourism posters and leaflets marked Dundee as a centre of whisky distillation but, contrary to popular belief and although many bottles of whisky over the years have carried the name, Dundee has never been a distilling centre of Scotland and any legal distillation is unlikely to have taken place there for over 150 years. However, many blending and distilling companies, such as Robertson and Son, did make it their home.

Artist: Arthur Clark

Date of registration: 3 Oct 1910

PRO reference: COPY 1/298 f 479

OLD HIGHLAND WHISKY

Once upon a time most brewers bought and blended their own Scotch. The now defunct Rochdale and Manor Brewery was just one of hundreds which sold their own whisky to the captive clientele of their tied houses. These whiskies were bought by the barrel from whisky merchants or from distilleries themselves and breweries would have employed an internal blender - sometimes the head brewer - who would have married together the malt and the grain. His duties would have extended to rum and brandy also. Their advertising was sometimes understandably without frills: just the bottle, the age and a scattering of thistles to leave no doubt as to the country of origin of the golden spirit. The artist of this example also designed artwork for the company's beer.

Today the number of brewers who still carry out this tradition can be counted on fingers. You might find pubs that sell their own brands, such as Holts of Manchester and Charles Wells of Bedford. But these are blended for them by independent blending and bottling companies. One exception to the rule is Eldridge Pope, the Dorchester brewers who have had whisky specially filled for them for over a century. Their 'The Chairman's' brand, one of my favourites, is blended exclusively from malt matured in sherry cask and contains only 40% grain. Like the RMB Old Highland whisky it is 8 years old. But Charles Wells' Red Seal tops that with a 12-year-old.

Artist: Arthur Clough
Date of registration: 26 February 1910
PRO reference: COPY 1/ 290 f 36

CHESTERS' FINE OLD SPECIAL WHISKIES

For all the good humour, here is a vivid example of how times and advertising values have changed. This poster, also commissioned by a brewery, breaks the cardinal rule which today governs whisky advertising: do not on any account make its appeal to the older generation.

Sales in dark spirits have fallen in Britain over the last two decades as traditional whisky drinkers have died off and the new generation which has taken their place has been weaned on a diet of relatively tasteless lager and vodka. Subsequently distillers have been trying to win over new converts, but so far with limited success. Such is the bowing to youth culture in Britain that no bourbon marketed here now uses the word 'Old' in its title, contrary to Kentucky tradition (even Old Forester brought out a new brand called Forester 1870) and when United Distillers launched their new RX brand they omitted the word 'whiskey' from anywhere on the label and referred to it simply as Bourbon. Such is the present state of paranoia.

The whisky this charming old Mancunian is carefully inspecting was blended by the lost and greatly lamented Chesters brewery which was closed by Whitbread in the 1980s. My local at the time, The Land o' Cakes, was a Chesters pub and although their own whisky (or whiskies as they preferred to call it) had vanished by the time I began drinking there in 1982, I did meet some old-timers who remembered the brand with affection.

Artist: Charles Lee
Date of registration: 31 January 1907
PRO reference: COPY 1 / 254 f 409

ROBERTSON'S DUNDEE WHISKY

If ever there was a whisky poster the temperance movement welcomed with open arms, this must be it. At the time of this advertisement prohibitionists were enjoying something of a revival, although nothing like so successfully as in the United States. One can only suspect that the artist, the whisky poster veteran Arthur Clark, must have been a recent convert or at least teetotal or a shareholder with Typhoo. Or still have a bill outstanding from one of his previous clients.

The sunken face, grey, sickly complexion and rosy glow of his cheeks suggests that this late night reveller drinks this whisky not so much for fun and enjoyment but from necessity. How any distilling company could imagine that such a sad and unhealthy figure could possibly be an endorsement to their product is beyond understanding, even taking into account the change in society values over the passing century or so. Perhaps they should have gone the whole way and tagged it 'Go on - finish yourself off'.

Ironically, the respected Dundee blenders and distillers, John Robertson, make a point of providing a certificate of analysis on the bottle to confirm its purity. Such an assurance though would have been of little import to the man who appears to be taking on the bottle single-handed in an age when the standard strength of whisky was approximately the same as direct from the cask, usually anything up to 57.1% alcohol by volume (100 proof Sikes), nearly 50% stronger than it is today.

Artist: Arthur Clark
Date of registration: 13 July 1904
PRO reference: COPY 1 / 218 f 371

ROBIN OIG FINE OLD SCOTCH WHISKY

This charming poster tells us more about the history of scotch whisky than it does about the little known company which produced this now obsolete brand. Again we have an advertisement that offers a distinctive class structure to promote a whisky. Rather than top hats and tails, we have those in the First Class compartment getting one up on those watching, not without an obvious tinge of jealousy, from the Second Class carriage. And again the recipients are officers in full military regalia.

This is quite significant because above their heads is the word Leith, the address of George Beer, the blenders of the whisky saving the day. Leith, an old port beside Edinburgh, has long been vital to the whisky industry. From the eighteenth century it was there that whisky was bonded and then 'exported' to England by sea. At that time there were different taxation rates on spirits made north and south of the border. This changed in the early 1820s but Leith, along with Aberdeen and Dundee in particular became vital as a centre of bonding and then export to overseas markets throughout the empire and to North America. With so much whisky being held in Leith warehouses, it was natural for blending companies, large and small, to gravitate there to set up office. The company depicted above was evidently small Beer.

Artist: William Pottle
Date of registration: 2 March 1898
PRO reference: COPY 1/139 f 113

FRASER'S OLD SCOTCH WHISKY

Over the last decade, distillers have begun pointing out in their advertising how their whisky is matured. It all began with The Macallan celebrating the fact that their Speyside single malt was bottled only if it had been matured in sherry casks, usually oloroso.

Since then there has been the phenomenon of 'finishing'. This means that the whisky would be matured mostly in ex-bourbon barrels before being transferred into sherry, madeira, port or even French wine casks for rounding off. For anything from six months to three years the whisky would gain extra flavours imparted by the wines.

This otherwise rather unimaginative poster makes a point of revealing that the whisky was matured in sherry wood. Few blenders at the time bothered to note this as sherry cask maturation was much more common than it is today. At the turn of the century all whisky would have been matured in casks that brought other spirits and wines into Britain. However, this changed after the second world war when the oak from which these barrels were made became rarer and more expensive. Also, sherry either arrived by tanker or pre-bottled. It was the Americans who came to the Scotch distillers' rescue. By law bourbon must be matured in virgin oak casks and once used are useless to the bourbon and rye industry. So it is no surprise when distillers today boast of using sherry casks: they are around ten times more expensive to buy than bourbon casks.

Sadly for Frasers of Dunfermline, they were nothing like as successful as The Macallan in impressing customers. The company and three brands have vanished without trace.

Artist: Charles Beauvais
Date of registration: 6 July 1899
PRO reference: COPY 1/154 f 467

RODERICK DHU

At the turn of the century Roderick Dhu was one of the most popular Scotch whiskies in Britain. And the year 1899 turned out to be a significant one for the brand's owners Wright and Greig. Despite the failure of Pattison and so much whisky sloshing around on the market, (something in the region of 90 million gallons), one of the most indomitable whisky speculators of his day, Alexander Edward, still decided to go ahead and build yet another distillery.

He called it Dallas Dhu and the following year he sold it to Wright and Greig who until that time had depended on Highland Park for much of its malt whisky. Dallas Dhu still stands today in the town of Forres, between Elgin and Inverness, in excellent condition but silent. It is the only government-owned distillery in Scotland, though it is used as a museum rather than for distillation: a pity for this was the producer of one of Scotland' s finest drams until it ceased production in 1983.

As you can see, once more a Scotch whisky poster depends upon the military, in this instance a Highlander, and though the concept of the freezing sentry having constantly to march past the vision of a bottle of whisky is cruelly clever, the punch-line has been entirely wasted.

Artist: Tom Browne
Date of registration: 20 June 1898
PRO reference: COPY 1/142 f 139

J & G STEWART' S GOLD MEDAL

The entering of competitions and winning of medals was once regarded by distillers as a good deal more important than it is today. Distillers such as Jack Daniel of Tennessee would personally travel thousands of miles to enter his whiskey into competition in the hope of striking gold. And when he did he would take full advantage of it on his advertising and labelling. Here, the famous old Edinburgh whisky house of J&G Stewart have gone one better and even named a brand after a local success.

Stewart's were among Edinburgh's finest and most respected whisky merchants, originally set up by James Stewart in 1779 as tea and wine importers. Once James was succeeded by his sons John and George, the Stewarts quickly established themselves as exporters of provisions, including whisky. Indeed, J&G Stewart were always better known for their export rather than home trade and when they were taken over by Distillers Company Ltd in 1917 vast stocks of whisky swelled the giant company's portfolio, despite the fact that J&G Stewart had never bought or built their own distillery.

By the time this poster was designed, the company was no longer a family concern and had moved into old premises once owned by the disgraced Pattisons. The Gold Medal brand may have vanished but the Stewart name, now part of United Distillers and Vintners, lives on as the licensee of Usher's Green Stripe, and with the blend, the curiously named Stewart's Vatted Scotch.

Artist: Arthur Hall
Date of registration: 16 November 1911
PRO reference: COPY 1/272i f 2

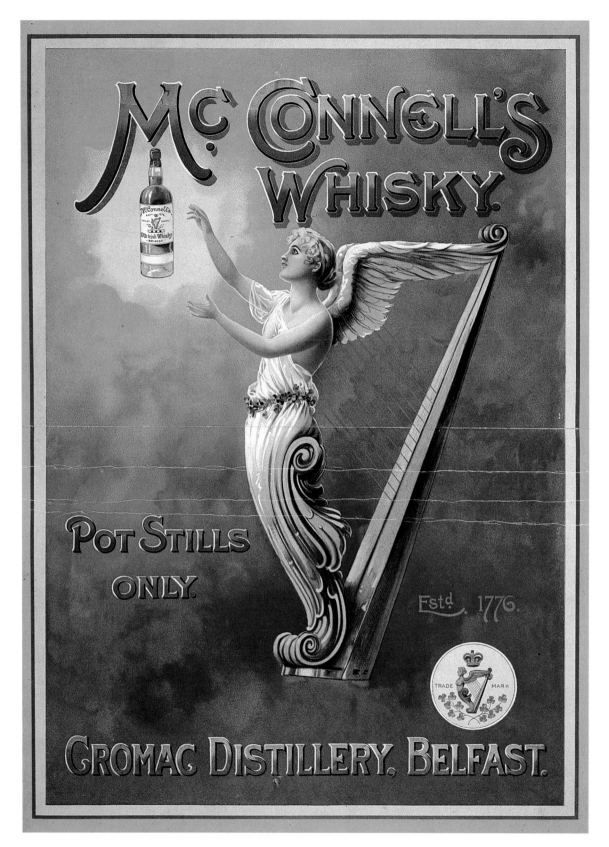

McCONNELL'S WHISKY

The Cromac Distillery was one of three or four operating from Belfast and its environs at the time of this majestic poster. With the harp, the shamrocks and this vision of loveliness in Erin it might be thought that this was a Catholic distillery in a Protestant stronghold. All Ireland was then still part of Great Britain and allegiance to king and country is evident from the crown above the harp in the bottom right hand corner and also by the spelling of 'whisky' without the 'e'. This is still referred to as the Protestant way of spelling Irish whiskey.

For the whiskey connoisseur, though, most absorbing is the term 'Pot Stills Only'. This not only means that the distillers have eschewed the practice of continuous distillation but suggests their whisky was a mixture of malted and unmalted barley. Old Bushmills, by contrast, always made a point of boasting they were 'Pure Malt' distillers. Confusingly, however, McConnell's, the owners of Cromac, also used the term 'Pot Still' whisky for their Stromness Highland Distillery on Orkney, but called that 'Pure Malt' as well.

The Cromac distillery was also rather unusual in being attached to J.J. McConnell's brewery, though a visit to the site of Corporation Street where brewery and distillery once stood side by side reveals today no evidence of either, the business having failed during the depression.

However, if the whiskey was anything like as beautiful as the poster designed to promote it, this must have been one of Ireland's very finest. But unless someone contacts me with an unopened bottle, it is unlikely I will ever know.

Artist: Howard Davie
Date of registration: 24 August 1898
PRO reference: COPY 1/143 i f 87

"STRATHMILL" WHISKY

"FROM THE ALPS TO THE ANDES."

This sketch shows some of W. & A. Gilbey's cases being transported on the backs of Llamas across the high plains of the Bolivian Andes (near Uyuni) at an altitude of 12,000 feet.

STRATHMILL WHISKY

Where the majority of exotic advertising art is based on fantasy or at least wishful thinking, this remarkable poster is based on fact. When it was commissioned in 1904 the Gilbey name had spread far and wide across the globe. And one of the more impressive destinations for their whisky was the continent of South America, where it even reached outposts high in the Andes.

The journey had started in other, more modest, Highlands, those of Speyside at the attractive Strathmill distillery in Keith. The whisky would then be brought down by train to Camden Town, London, where beside the Regent's Canal the malt would be bottled and cased before being sent on a special train, the 'Gilbey Special' which each day would pull out of Camden to one of various ports.

The whisky would then be shipped all over the world including South America. This particular poster depicts the whisky being transported by llamas across the high plains of the Bolivian Andes at an altitude of no less than 12,000 feet near Uyuni. The llama train carrying whisky is a thing of the past, but Strathmill continues to this day producing one of Scotland's most delicate malts.

Artist: Harry Rowntree
Date of registration: 14 April 1904
PRO reference: COPY 1/215ii f 266

DEWAR'S WHISKY

Works in the manner of Old Masters are most unusual for whisky advertising, but around 1905 Dewar's commissioned a number of artists to create works in a style more likely to have found a home in an art gallery than on a poster hoarding or the pages of a magazine. The style of Henry Gillard's 'The Shipwreck' is perhaps of a genre favoured more by designers of biscuit tins than of whisky packaging or advertising.

Of course, Dewar's were claiming by implication that their famous blended whisky was an Old Master in its own right. However, for this poster with two men about to take issue over who owns the flask containing the coveted Dewar's, one might think that rum would have been the favoured drink. At the time that this little skirmish on the shore was taking place, the name 'whisky' was still unknown to the world. The characters seem to date from earlier than the end of the eighteenth century and if had been whisky they were after they would have known it better as *uisge beatha, aqua vitae* or simply malt spirit.

Artist: Henry Gillard
Date of registration: 16 November 1905
PRO reference: COPY 1/235i f 362

DEWAR'S CEMENT THE QUARREL

This clever and romanticised vision of bygone Scottish life stems from the imagination of Buckinghamshire artist George Herbert Jupp. Called 'Cement the Quarrel' the painting depicts two members of opposing clans meeting in a flagstoned inn and putting aside their differences over a dram, of course. Naturally, one assumes the whisky is Dewar's, though quite rarely for any advertising artwork the name of the whisky is nowhere to be seen. Only the statement that it was published by John Dewar and Sons Ltd reveals the poster's intention.

It is plain that this poster and others in the same serious style were intended to give a clear message that Dewar's were to be regarded as a little more up-market than other less tasteful rival companies. This emphasis on quality is used to reflect benevolently on the whisky.

It is no great surprise that Dewar's took a greater interest than most in art as advertising. In 1904 the energetic and legendary head of the company, Tommy Dewar, published his memoirs of selling Dewar's to an unsuspecting world, called *A Ramble Round the Globe*. He used eight artists to illustrate the book, including Phil May who three years later designed a series of postcards for Dewar's which are now collectors' items.

Artist: George Herbert Jupp
Date of registration: 16 February 1905
PRO reference: COPY 1/226i f 332

CEMENT THE QUARREL. *(Copyright.)*

Published by John Dewar & Sons, Ltd., Perth, Scotland and London.

IONA

The names of Hebridean islands have always been synonymous with Scotch whisky. Even today single malt whisky is still legally produced on Islay, Jura, Skye, Mull and Arran.

However, commercial distillers have always avoided the tiny island of Iona near Mull where, if legend is true, illegal distillers and smugglers took a greater interest. Iona is better known for its religious links, having been a stopping point for St. Columba when he decided to leave Ireland for Scotland in 563, taking with him, as some Irish claim without any foundation whatsoever, the secret of whisky making. For St. Columba was a holy man as opposed to a distiller; because of the island's spirituality a succession of Scottish kings was buried there.

The spirit pursued by the Scotsman in this attractive poster is of a much baser kind. He is drinking a blend that has been given the name simply for its fame, and grain whisky is something that has never been made on any Hebridean island. The designers of this advertisement have picked out the red and yellow colours of the label, using them very effectively to form a striking and unusual image. Perhaps the bottlers, the Maclachans, were followers of the Glasgow soccer club Partick Thistle, whose colours of red and yellow match those on the bottle and who a few years earlier had been runners up in the Scottish Second Division.

Artists: Alfred Pearce, Arthur Buchanan and John Hull
Date of registration: 19 November 1907
PRO reference: COPY 1/263 f 224

STRATHMILL

The London firm of W. A. Gilbey began life in 1857 when two brothers, fresh from the Crimean war where they had served in the pay department near Gallipoli, formed a modest wine merchant business. It was another thirty years before they began selling whisky to any great extent and in 1887 they bought the Glen Spey distillery in Rothes. Their second distillery was Strathmill, and a year before this artwork was commissioned Gilbey had also invested in a third Speyside distillery, Knockando.

This poster, with its faint echoes of *Whisky Galore*, was unusual at that time because it was then very rare for single malt whisky to be openly advertised. The directors of Gilbey had ignored the possibilities of blending whisky on the grounds that customers should be left in no doubt as to exactly what kind of whisky they were buying. However just months after this poster was copyrighted Gilbey at last bought stocks of grain whisky in order to satisfy what they were recognising as public demand for a lighter style of dram.

It appears that the poster's punchline, 'The Only Thing Worth Saving' was not quite as glib as it first seems. On 25 November 1992 a bottle of Strathmill from around the date of the poster fetched £2,500 at Christie's in Glasgow, a then record for a standard non-vintage bottle of whisky.

Artist: Charles Lee
Date of registration: 18 February 1905
PRO reference: COPY 1/226i f 311

ARTHUR BELL AND SONS

It is rare that an artwork can be linked to any single individual within a whisky company through its style alone, but that is certainly the case here. This remarkably life-like image of a Scotsman curling is down to one man alone: A K Bell.

It was his father, Arthur Bell, who in 1851 founded what is now one of the most famous whisky names in the world. He had served his apprenticeship in Perth with Sandemans. When he set out alone, or to be precise with James Roy, a business partner and friend, he had no place in his tightly run ship for wasteful expenditure such as advertising. It was only after his death in 1900 that the name and reputation of Bell's spread faster than by word of mouth alone.

His son Arthur Kinmond Bell was a great sports enthusiast, his favourite being cricket, in which he even went on to captain Perthshire. He obviously recognised the link between healthy outdoor Scottish pursuits such as curling or golf (and probably cricket) and whisky.

Whether this was initially designed as a poster, showcard or label is open to debate. It was used as the label for Bell's whisky later the same year. Whatever the intention of this artwork, one of the most remarkable facts is that it was the first ever to use the name Arthur Bell.

Artist: William Trotter
Date of registration: 22 April 1904
PRO reference: COPY 1/215 f 280

Six years after the curling enthusiast was commissioned, A K Bell returned to Edinburgh-based artist William Trotter with a request for him to continue his effective work. It is noticeable here, though, that the sportsman wielding the wood is much younger than the curler. Curiously, in the mid 1990s Bell's made a concerted effort to win over younger drinkers and from the evidence of this drawing from 1910 it appears that history was repeating itself.

In the intervening six years Bell's had grown steadily as a company. But it was not until 1922 that the golfer found himself as the label for Bell's whisky. Oddly, it gives the date of establishment as 1825. That was the year Sandeman, for whom Arthur Bell and James Roy worked, set up business in Perth.

At the time of this artwork Bell's was a proud Scottish independent still without its own distillery. Two were bought in 1933, Blair Athol and Dufftown. Inchgower, Pittyvaich and Bladnoch were added to the stable before Bell's was bought by Guinness in 1987. Today it is part of the giant Diageo food and drinks company.

Artist: William Trotter
Date of registration: 15 December 1910
PRO reference: COPY 1/301 f 155

OLD ORKNEY SPECIAL SCOTCH

One of the most charming of all the whisky posters held at the Public Record Office is this amusing offering from Stromness Distillery. Had it been drawn in black and white rather than vivid pastel and an Irishman substituted for the Scotsman it might have been a scene from Will Hay's 'Oh Mr. Porter!' It predates 'O.O. is Needed in London' (see page 22) by only a year, but its style is far more old-fashioned. A change of artist may have resulted in a more immediately striking poster but clearly did little to make the brand seem more warm and appealing.

The Stromness distillery was built in 1817 and between 1825 and 1831 was in competition with another distillery half a mile or so north of the town. However, it saw off its rival and continued until closure in 1928. For a short while it was known as The Man o' Hoy Distillery in recognition of its close proximity to that dramatic rock face and was itself built into the side of a hill so most of the distilling processes were gravity fed. With its two tiny 300-gallon stills, one of them once belonging to an illicit distiller, it was a distillery which particularly fascinated Alfred Barnard during his travels to all Britain's distilleries in the 1880s and he had no hesitation in declaring it 'the most remote Distillery in the Kingdom.'

Artists: Edward Holliday and John Ellerton
Date of registration: 27 October 1905
PRO reference: COPY 1/234 f 386

ROYAL CLUB BLEND

Yet another poster to reinforce the idea that all Scotsmen during the late Victorian and early Edwardian era had orange beards. Advertisers of the time paid more attention to the detail of the people who drank their whisky than to the whisky itself. These days the idea is to get the message across as to what kind of character you will find in the glass: smoky, honeyed, mellow and so on. In 1908 the only way to have a clue was to purchase and open a bottle.

The artist, it is not difficult to believe, lived in West Hampstead, hence the unconvincing attempt at a Scots accent. And to further support the Scottish atmosphere, what better than to rely upon the sport that the Scots gave the world, golf?

The blender, Hyams, was also London-based and vanished like a ball in the rough. However, the Royal Club name did live on into the 1970s before being lost amid a number of takeovers and mergers. Although I could find no trace of the whisky being available today, it just might still be out on the course somewhere.

Artist: Andrew Maclure
Date of registration: 19 February 1908
PRO reference: COPY 1/ 266 f 165

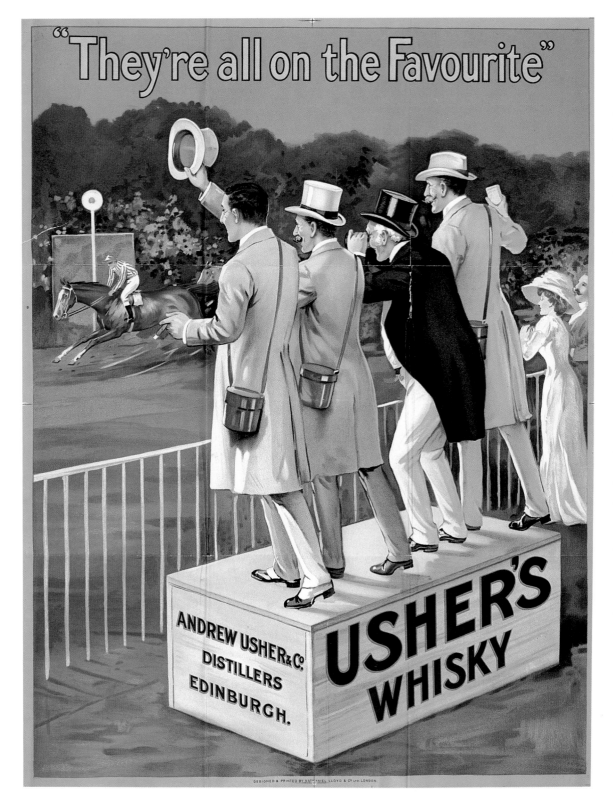

USHER'S WHISKY

Sporting events became an increasingly popular theme for distillers and blenders to focus on as the battle for supremacy in the markets hotted up. It is curious to note, however, that although much whisky was drunk by the working classes, advertising such as this was geared toward the well-to-do who are always handsomely depicted. The four gentlemen enjoying their day at the races are every bit as likely to own the horse they are cheering as merely to have backed it.

Another interesting point about this poster is that it forms the subtlest brand advertising found in this book. Outwardly the advertisement appears to be pushing the name of the distiller, in this case Andrew Usher. One of their principal brands was Usher's Green Stripe, which just happens to be the favours of the jockey. The catch line 'They're all on the Favourite' then becomes an even more clever choice of wording. This form of advertising shows great confidence on the part of Ushers who eight years later were bought out by the Distillers Company Ltd. Green Stripe can still be drunk today, but normally you would have to go to South America to find it. While there you might take in some llama racing.

Artist: Robert Hepple
Date of registration: 24 April 1911
PRO reference: COPY 1/ 306 f 105

REAL MOUNTAIN DEW

It is hard to imagine today a whisky company, or indeed any company, selecting a politician as a role model for their brand. But there was not quite the same cynicism pervading society in 1911, a time of relative peace and calm before two catastrophic world wars and the advent of biting satire and lack of faith in politicans. It is also noticeable from the caption: 'Gentlemen – Our Oldest Member' that the women were regarded as fit neither to hold political office nor drink whisky.

But people elected to drink Real Mountain Dew. The brand was popular enough to see in the 1960s and the Dundee blenders W&S Strong were in a secure enough financial position in 1964 to join ranks with fellow whisky brokers Hay & Macleod in the building of the Tomintoul-Glenlivet distillery in Speyside, one of the best whisky-producing plants built during the 1960s. Both companies held a half share. In 1973 Scottish and Universal Investment Trust took it over, who in turn were swallowed by Whyte and Mackay. They still own the Real Mountain Dew brand name but the blend is no longer marketed.

Artist: Arthur Kyle
Date of registration: 16 November 1911
PRO reference: COPY 1/315ii f 6

GLEN SPEY PURE MALT

From a purely whisky writer's angle, this has to be my favourite poster in this book. Not only does it have an exceptionally clear view of the bottle and all its details regarding the strength of the whisky inside, but the artist has been allowed to draw the Glen Spey distillery in all its beauty. To be exact, there is more beauty in the painting than there was in real life. Whilst the distillery was of these proportions and was situated beside the Burn of Rothes as it tumbles towards the Spey, it did not enjoy quite the country location depicted, being on the outskirts of the town of Rothes.

It is also fascinating to note the design of the chimney atop the square malting kiln, at the front right of the distillery. In 1904 it was still of an unfussy utilitarian style which fulfilled its purpose of allowing the smoke to rise from the kiln, pass through the drying malted barley and into the Speyside air. Very soon after this the chimney was altered, purely for decorative reasons, to the pagoda style which is now common throughout Scotland. The Glen Spey distillery still operates today as part of UDV, making a malt which is a vital constituent part of the J&B brand.

Artist: Ernest Bertram

Date of registration: 14 November 1904

PRO reference: COPY 1/223i f 330

FORRES BLEND

Once more a horsy theme takes to the saddle for the pushing of a blend whisky. And the artist, Nottingham-based Isaac Cullen, has taken full advantage of the opportunity to make a portrait of a thoroughbred as life-like as possible, perhaps inspired by the nationally famed horse and hunting scene artist John Ferneley who had lived and worked in nearby Melton Mowbray, Leicestershire. It goes without saying that the inference, and indeed the witty copy, is to leave no one in doubt that the blend is a thoroughbred, too.

The whisky, like the artist, is also from that area served by the London and Midland line to St. Pancras. Hay and Son were based in the steel-making town of Sheffield, though a contemporary Bond Book, in which a Sheffield company listed every individual barrel of whisky they held in stock, does not mention Hay as one of their customers. Since this poster dates from 1908 and the whisky is 11 years of age, we can safely discount the Forres distillery of Dallas Dhu being a constituent of the blend as it was built in only 1899; likewise the other Forres distillery, Benromach, which was not opened until 1898. Perhaps it included some Glenburgie, which is situated in the nearby village of Alves and was going strong when the blend' s whisky was made, as it

still is today. Or maybe it had none of these and Hay and Son just liked the name 'Forres'.

Artist: Isaac Cullen
Date of registration: 17 July 1908
PRO reference: COPY 1/271 f 136

ROYAL ARMS SCOTCH

This poster, dated 1911, is similar to a number of humorous postcards doing the rounds at that time. Unlike the postcards, which could refer to any blend, the name of the whisky is here clearly defined. With the caption: 'Here's Luck to the Boss', it looks like a servant helping himself to a sly one. However, according to the original description written by the artist, John Lloyd, the man is actually a waiter, which deflates the joke somewhat.

The company behind the brand, J.G. Thomson of Leith, was one of Scotland's oldest commercial concerns and, at the time of this poster, growing into one of the most powerful whisky companies in Scotland. Dating back to 1709 it eventually attracted none other than Andrew Usher who in 1875 bought into the company. In 1919 the company teamed up with those other formidable Edinburgh blenders, Charles Mackinlay, to buy the now silent Littlemill lowland distillery. Just two years later J.G. Thomson were effectively ended as a force when DCL bought out all their whisky stocks, but not the company which eventually melted away.

Their old address of The Vaults, Leith, dating right back to 1709, is likely to ring a bell with the most serious whisky connoisseur: it is today the impressive home of The Scotch Malt Whisky Society who supply to members single malt whisky direct from the cask.

Artist: John Lloyd
Date of registration: 25 January 1911
PRO reference: COPY 1/302 f 138

TEACHER'S SCOTCH WHISKY

Here is a blend that is instantly recognisable, having survived unscathed the test of time like so few others, with a label whose simple, virtually unaltered style is still known the world over. The calendar may be for 1906 (and note from the line through it that it was felt they could not copyright the year as well!) but in some ways the advertisement could be for 1996.

One major difference is that Teacher's is now part of the vast Allied Domecq empire. Then it was a fiercely independent family company and did not succumb to takeover until 1976. It could easily have done so 55 years earlier when the predatory DCL coveted Teacher's enormous whisky stocks. Instead, and luckily for whisky drinkers today, they bought J.G. Thomson's. Teacher's claim their year of establishment as 1830, probably the date William Teacher began work at his eventual in-laws' grocery and then spirit business.

Recent years have seen a slight decline in Teacher's sales, but it still accounts for around two million cases of whisky annually. Then, like today, the blend benefited from having an above average amount of malt in its make-up. And just as in 1906, an important constituent malt is from their own Ardmore distillery, producer of one of the most distinctive smoky spirits on mainland Scotland.

Artist: Tom Browne
Date of registration: 2 October 1905
PRO reference: COPY 1/234 f 504

OLD DAD SCOTCH WHISKY

The punchline 'An Open Door May Tempt a Saint' gives an amusing tag to this delightful poster dating back to 1904. And one can't help wondering: is the priest being tempted by the whisky or the barmaid? Or both?

There is little that can be said about the whisky as it has long since been shunted into the sidings. And of the blenders there is equally little trace. But at least for those in search of that kind of thing, there is an all too obvious spelling mistake, where 'Down Line' on the bulletin board timetable actually reads 'Down Lime.'

A curiosity is that on the original document a little of the writing is in German. The artist may well have been German and perhaps was not entirely familiar with English, which might explain the spelling mistake. At least the strength of the drawing is that the joke can stand alone, even without the help of a punchline.

Artist: Victor Verner
Date of registration: 23 August 1904
PRO reference: COPY 1/219 f 175

"A NATIONAL DRAW."

ROYAL LIQUEUR WHISKY

It is noticeable from many of the posters of this period that distillers sometimes called their blend 'liqueur whisky'. Under no circumstances should this be confused with 'whisky liqueur', which is another thing entirely. The term 'liqueur whisky' was used merely to imply that the spirit was of a high quality and should be enjoyed at leisure. It had not undergone any special ageing, nor had any compounds been added to alter its flavour. A whisky liqueur, on the other hand, is a spirit sweetened and flavoured with honey, herbs and spices and uses whisky from any country as the base spirit.

Here the little known company of Bothwell made a point of returning whisky back to perhaps the reason monks made it in the first place: for medicinal purposes. Here we see two senior officers being administered the prescribed elixir or 'ancient stimulant' by the matron. And in the next caption they are both right as ninepence; 'Both-well' to be exact!

These days it is not easy to find a whisky dubbed as liqueur. It not quite extinct but certainly an endangered species.

Artist: James Thorpe
Date of registration: 22 February 1909
PRO reference: COPY 1 / 278 f 81

OLD DAD

This second Old Dad poster is also from 1904, but, being registered at the Stationers' Hall on 16 December, arrived four months later. Here the company has switched tack and artist. Still on the humorous side, Angas and Co. have pulled away from a topic that could have been regarded just a little controversial and plumped for stereotype.

Heard the one about the Scotsman, the Irishman and Englishman? They are all there, in national garb, though it seems slightly unfair that John Bull has been allowed to bring his dog while there is no sign of an Irish setter or a Scottish terrier. There is something slightly familiar about our friend John Bull. This work is the creation of Arthur Clark who six years earlier did such an attractive job on the Friar Royd poster (page 17). The centre monk in that picture has a similar cherubic look to the Englishman here. And if you look at some of Clark's later work, in this case Robertson's Yellow Label from six years further on (page 28), you will notice a similar rosy face peering down from a horse. It is hard to believe that just five months earlier he had been responsible for the deathly Robertson poster on page 31.

Artist: Arthur Clark, London
Date of registration: 16 December 1904
PRO reference: COPY 1/224 f 136

Royal Liqueur Whisky

★ ★ ★ ★

Ancient Stimulant.

Doctor's Orders

"Both-well"

Selected & Bottled by The **Bothwell Bonding Co.,**

GLASGOW.

"FIRESIDE"

BLEND

Old Vatted

TRADE  MARK

GLENLIVET WHISKY

SOLE PROPRIETORS
Massey's Burnley Brewery Ltd BURNLEY.

SIR JOSEPH CAUSTON & SONS, LIMITED, DESIGNERS & PRINTERS, LONDON.

FIRESIDE BLEND

Considering that this was a blended whisky designed exclusively for the good people of Burnley, Lancashire, one can only admire the effort undertaken by Massey's Brewery in 1904 to win over converts.

Today the image would be thrown out of court by every advertising agency – and probably distiller – in the land. That snug, middle-aged vision of people enjoying a dram by a roaring fire (or inferno, in this case) would set the industry back decades.

One interesting point is Massey's terminology. Having already declared their whisky a blend they confuse matters somewhat by calling it Old Vatted. Vatting is now a term commonly used for mixing malt whiskies together from different distilleries. So a vatted

malt is not a single malt, nor a blend, but a pure malt from more than one distillery. However, at the time of this poster, to vat usually meant mixing whiskies from the same distillery but of different ages. So what is believed to be the first blend, Usher's Vatted Glenlivet, probably began life as what we would now regard a single malt but eventually had grain whisky added to it. The artist Charles Lee designed posters for other brewers (see page 30). The rich colour and strong design sense evident in this poster was enough to ensure a commission the following year to design an advertisement for the large and powerful company of W A Gilbey (page 40).

Artist: Charles Lee

Date of registration: 16 April 1904

PRO reference: COPY 1/215 f 301

THE WORLD'S BEST

Stirring stuff from J G Thomson, that proud old Edinburgh whisky company who obviously took their seafaring base at Leith very seriously indeed. Doubtless the Royal Warrant they had received from King Edward VII did much to focus their minds on the Empire.

This style of artwork is a dramatic departure from what we have come to expect from the artist William Trotter. It was he who created the two famous Arthur Bell images of the the curler and the golfer. This calendar was lodged at Stationers' Hall on 23 December 1907, apparently far too late to send it out to customers worldwide by January 1. However, designs were often registered in batches, sometimes months after being commissioned and used, so this

may well have been dispatched weeks before.

When it arrived, for Scottish expatriates at least, the impressive sight of that monument to railway engineering, the Forth Bridge, just 17 years old at the time, and a couple of bottles of whisky must have been every bit as heartening as the might of the Royal Navy.

Artist: William Trotter

Date of registration: 23 December 1907

PRO reference: COPY 1/264 f 35

SUPREMACY SCOTCH WHISKY

The London artist John Lloyd was popular among whisky advertising agencies for his light-hearted work. An example we have is the Royal Arms waiter poster (page 49). But the message he has been asked to get across here is something more serious: the link between the sturdy farmer back home and the brave, noble officers of His Majesty's forces protecting the British Empire.

Even the title of the whisky, 'Supremacy', has a jingoistic ring about it. The farmer stands proudly by a greatly aged whisky and to reinforce the feel of Britain's precious soil, and indeed perhaps in a bid to almost cruelly remind soldiers of it, it appears the whisky has been packed in boxes lined with sheaves of Scottish barley. Although the Glasgow blenders George Ballantine were then also promoting whisky of a similar age, this is the oldest whisky, at 21 years

old, for which an advertisement was lodged at the Stationers' Hall. As well as this poster, a second dated 20 June 1904 was lodged with exactly the same characters standing in the same pose but the whisky depicted was 'Ye O.H.M. Whisky distilled in ye Highlands of Scotland'. There is also a lot more barley around on the second poster.

Not surprisingly, like the Empire, both brands, as well as R H Hall, have been lost to us. But the poster serves as a vivid reminder of how distillers sometimes sponsored regiments by sending them whisky as a morale booster, especially at times of conflict.

Artist: John Lloyd
Date of registration: 20 June 1904
PRO reference: COPY 1/ 220 ii f 87

BEGORRA IT'S COWAN'S

Some posters make you wince and this is one. First you have the 'begorra'! Next you have the cloned Irishman with what the artist apparently believed to be the only style of clothing people on the beautiful isle ever wore. Then you have the crown on the cask to leave no-one in any doubt what side of the political division that company is sitting on. And finally you have about the biggest piece of blarney you will ever read: 'Recommended by the leading Medical Faculty as the purest whisky in the world.'

It rather defies belief that this unnamed faculty has actually been able to sample every whisky being made at that time, not just in the British Isles but also from Kentucky to Australia. This poster was probably intended to impress drinkers in Cowan's export markets, such as the USA, rather than those at home.

William Cowan was not a distiller. But he had a good choice

of local distilleries from which to buy his whisky. The most likely was the Royal Irish Distilleries, better known as Dunville's. The poster makes no mention of pot stills so it is possible that Cowan might have bought in grain whisky from the United Distilleries plants at Connswater and Avoniel in and around Belfast.

Artist: William Wilson
Date of registration: 2 August 1899
PRO reference: COPY 1/155 f 403

JOHN JAMESON WHISKEY

1998 marks the thirtieth anniversary of the most famous Irish distillers of them all, John Jameson and Son, bottling their own whiskey for the very first time. So how can we explain this superb poster for Jameson whiskey, not only registered at Stationers' Hall in 1906, but with the actual season the whiskey was made marked on the bottle?

The answer is quite simple. Until 1968 Jameson sold their whiskey by the barrel only. It was up to other distillers and whiskey merchants to bottle and sell the whiskey with their great name.

One of their biggest customers were the Scottish blenders W A Gilbey. So great was the demand for Gilbey's Irish whiskey that by the mid-1870s close on two out of every three bottles of whiskey they sold was Irish, though not all of it Jameson. From 1864 they had formed a close partnership for John Jameson to supply the Redbreast 12-year-old, a brand which stands today – though now under the Jameson flag – and Castle Grand JJ, the brand depicted here.

The label happens to have a very similar shape to the Powers Irish brand of today. It is interesting to note that in those days you could get a penny back on your bottle. This Jameson whiskey would have been 100% pure pot still, a mixture of malted and unmalted barley. The Bow Street distillery where it was made is now closed, though a brand new visitors' centre has been created there. Jameson pot still whiskey is now made at Midleton Distillery near Cork. And the good news is that after years of decline, Irish whiskey, headed by Jameson, is enjoying a healthy revival.

Artist: Ernest Bertram
Date of registration: 18 October 1906
PRO reference: COPY 1/ 250 f 462

BUCHANAN'S' BLACK & WHITE

When I wrote earlier in this book that James Buchanan was not a man to do things by halves, I had not yet stumbled across this advertisement from 1908. It was strikingly elegant and classical artwork like this, intermingled with other dazzling pieces of advertising, that kept his brand very much in the public eye, as we shall see later on (page 64). Here the bottle placed on a carved stone pedestal gives the whisky a feeling of both age and craftsmanship while the beauties flanking it with their garlands and robes of silk and velvet portray the values of the whisky when it is savoured. This is very serious advertising.

Against such a background of fine valued artwork it almost seems a shame that a move was gradually made towards animal designs, culminating with the two Scotties, one black, the other white, which adorn every bottle of Buchanan.

Such was James Buchanan's marketing success that in 1894 he even built a Speyside distillery to guarantee supplies for his blend. Ironically Glentauchers is now one of the finest distilleries owned by Allied Domecq, arch-rivals of Black and White's present blenders, United Distillers and Vintners.

Artist: Giovanni Barbaro
Date of registration: 23 July 1908
PRO reference: COPY 1/315i f 352

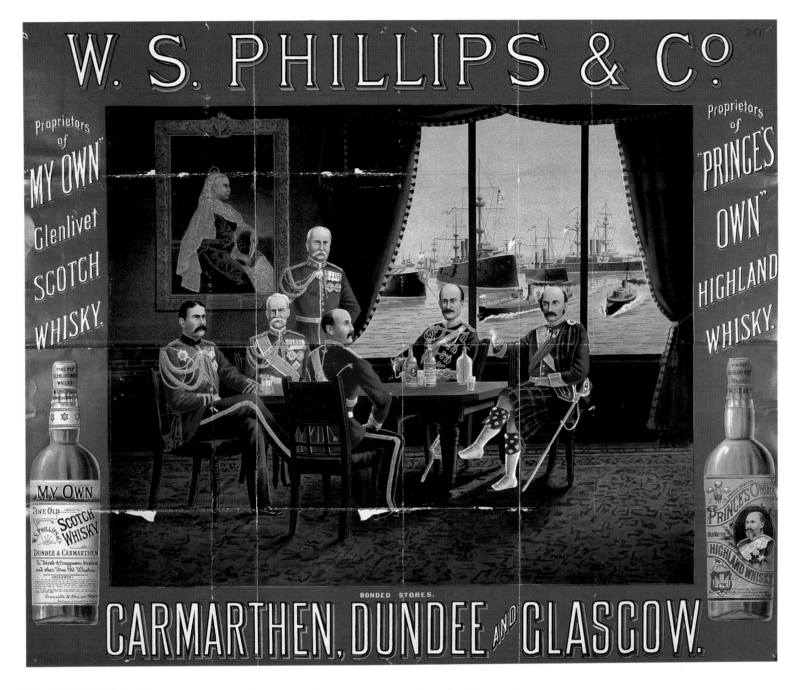

W.S. PHILLIPS & CO.

This is one of the most odd whisky posters I have ever come across. The six uniformed men of obvious rank and stature sitting and standing beyond the sober gaze of Queen Victoria are not just drawn from the imagination of artist Christian Fesch: they were all major personages of their time. Here we have no less than Generals Baden Powell (of Boy Scout fame), Kitchener (of Your Country Needs You), Kekewich and White with General Buller standing behind Field Marshal Lord Roberts.

It is not known whether all these prominent members of the

Establishment agreed to being used to promote the product of an otherwise obscure whisky blending company based in distant Wales. It seems highly unlikely. If they had, perhaps one should not be too surprised not to find General Haig amongst them! Each member of this august group appear to have had their heads drawn first and their bodies followed. The result is six models with heads out of proportion with the rest of their bodies.

As for the whisky, 'My Own' commands a great deal of respect. It boasts of containing that magnificent Speysider, Cragganmore, for a long time rated

the pride of the Distillers Company malt distilleries and now a member of the United Distillers and Vintners Class Malt range. One can't help feeling, however, that the senior generals wished it doubled as a hair restorer...

Artist: Christian Adolphus Fesch
Date of registration: 22 August 1900
PRO reference: COPY 1/ 169 f 251

FOUR CROWN WHISKY

In Scotland, there were distillers. Then there were those who called themselves distillers. Robert Brown appears to fall into the latter category. At the base of the poster it is quite clear: 'Sole Proprietors:- Robert Brown Ltd Distillers, Glasgow, Scotland.'

No such claim is made on the bottle but nevertheless Brown left no doubt they regarded themselves as distillers. However, having checked through all my own records, and double checked with those published by whisky historian Michael Moss, I can find no evidence at all that Robert Brown Ltd of Holm Street, Glasgow ever owned a distillery. They probably used the term on the strength that they ordered distillers to make it for them: in whisky parlance distilleries filled for them.

But Robert Brown was a company of substance. In 1910, the year before this poster, the company had celebrated its half century and though they owned no distillery they did possess two oak blending vats in which some 25,000 gallons of Four Crown whisky would mingle. The company and brand are both no more. They were bought out in 1935 by the giant Canadian distilling firm, Seagram. This was partly to acquire their large blending stocks but possibly above all for the Four Crown title: one of Seagram's biggest selling brands in North America was (and still is) Seven Crown.

The artwork for this brand is quite interesting. Here we can see a trend that had taken off in that the whisky would be served with a splash from a water syphon. Later this would be become a soda syphon so whisky and soda became a standard drink far more common than a straight whisky.

Artist: William Fry
Date of registration: 27 July 1911
PRO reference: COPY 1/310 f 45

TEACHER'S SCOTCH WHISKY

This is another of the prolific poster artist Tom Browne's delightful advertisements for Teacher's (see page 50). For a change the setting has been moved from Scotland to England, but with the obligatory orange-bearded Scot thrown in to be on the safe side. This poster dates from 1904 and here you can see the lady cradling Teacher's Highland Cream, a term that was officially adopted in 1884. It might be that this party are heading north to Glasgow, the bottle to keep them company. When they arrived they would have found scattered throughout the city a series of Teacher's 'dram shops'.

These unique premises arrived on the scene during the 1850s when William Teacher decided that rather than just sell whisky from his grocer's shop he would gain a licence for people to take a nip while there. Teacher's Dram Shops, each individually lettered, became an integral part of the Glasgow scene until their demise in the 1960s. Extraordinary as it may seem in today's society, at the time of this poster customers were allowed to buy a drink only for themselves, at threepence a nip, and if they wished to smoke they had to do so outside. Should they be showing signs of having had even a half too many, they would be forcibly marched outside and dissuaded from returning.

Artist: Tom Browne
Date of registration: 5 December 1904
PRO reference: COPY 1 / 224 f 370

MACKAY'S LIQUEUR WHISKY

A later poster from a blender now entirely lost to us appears to ape some of the humour of the Teacher's effort but with none of its charm.

The image of a young child smoking is not one that these days sends people scampering out to buy a bottle of a particular whisky, but things were different in 1911. A & B Mackay's message that their whisky is first seems to run parallel to Teacher's 'Always In Front' slogan. But the class divide and the threat of the whip also do little to make this a particularly attractive specimen of whisky advertising nearly ninety years on.

Once again we see the use of the term 'Liqueur Whisky' to make the blend appear better than it probably was.

Artist: Robert Douglas
Date of registration: 20 March 1911
PRO reference: COPY 1/ 305 f 159

BUCHANAN'S BLACK AND WHITE LEADS

Here is a head-on clash between two themes dear to the heart of whisky baron James Buchanan: horses and his beloved Black and White brand which made it possible for him to indulge in them.

Although this poster was not registered until 1900, the artist's mark clearly shows the date 1899. That was the year Buchanan entered into horse racing seriously when Little Red Rat won at Newmarket. Four years later he was to buy a large estate, Lavington Park in the Sussex Downs, which not only became his baronial home but also one of the world's leading stud farms. His racing colours, which were to be seen first past the post twice at the Derby (with Captain Cuttle, 1922, and Coronach, 1926) as well as the Cesarewitch, St Leger and the Eclipse Stakes, were not surprisingly black and white. This picture, however, concentrates on another form of equine sport, polo.

Buchanan eventually ended up as part of the DCL empire but not without a fight. In 1915 Buchanan merged with Dewar's to form Scotch Whisky Brands Ltd. Johnnie Walker, the last of the big three independents, declined to come on board. Ironically all three became part of DCL in 1925 where they remained together through the Scottish Malt Distillers and Guinness days until Dewar's was lost as part of the deal which brought together Guinness and Grand Metropolitan, whose whisky arm is today known as United Distillers and Vintners.

Artist: Alfred Chantrey Corbould
Date of registration: 23 January 1900
PRO reference: COPY 1/160 f 138

THREE PERFECT SCOTCH WHISKIES AND BROWN'S SPECIAL

These early colour advertisements, both dating from July 1895, depict perfectly the kind of whiskies that could be found around London during the late Victorian era.

J Brown and Co were located in unfashionable Stoke Newington and had appeared to have little reputation outside the capital. So a scatter-gun approach was used. One brand, Brown's Special, was used in the hope of the getting the company's name better known. But if people preferred to stick with old familiar names, then they had up their sleeve three further brands.

The first was a more expensive all malt brand called Duke of Cambridge, where the title is used to give a feel of nobility to the whisky; the centre bottle uses the term 'Old Glenlivet' despite it being a blend, simply because everyone had heard that whisky from the Glenlivet was regarded as of the highest quality; and the third was The Emperor, a brand which claims to be of special appointment to the Imperial Household, though it doesn't specify which one. These four whiskies, probably unadulterated, wonderfully typify the many thousands of brands that could be found at that time.

Artist: George Hayles
Date of registration: 30 July 1895
PRO reference: COPY 1/119 f 222 and f 223

BL SCOTCH WHISKY

For the whisky lover it is fascinating to speculate on what each of the individual brands tasted like all those years ago. Very few, if any, of the posters have made much of a point about how the whisky was flavoured. With Phillips' My Own whisky (page 60) at least we had the clue that Cragganmore was involved, though that being a complex Speysider it would have simply developed the character of the blend rather than dominated it. But with this blend from Bulloch, Lade & Co, it is much easier to imagine.

This is not because the brand has survived the intervening 87 years, but more to do with knowing which distilleries it used in the making of its whisky back in 1911. At that time Bulloch, Lade owned two distilleries. One was the now lost Camlachie lowland distillery which would have been used to bulk up the malt content. However, their whisky from Caol Ila on Islay would have been used sparingly, but enough I am sure to give the blend a distinctive, rich, smoky character and a matching aroma which is unhappily tantalising the ghillie. Bulloch, Lade date back to 1860 but in 1927 became part of the all-consuming DCL. Caol Ila still produces its peat-reeked malt today. It has since been rebuilt and the whisky made there now is a lot fatter and oilier in style than the Caol Ila of old. But it is comforting to know that it is still licensed in the name of Bulloch, Lade and Co.

Artist: John Hassall
Date of registration: 30 June 1911
PRO reference: COPY 1/310 f 382

RODERICK DHU OLD HIGHLAND WHISKY

This jolly poster from Tom Browne in 1901 shows the dying rays of Victorian style in women's fashion and architecture. But more importantly it displays a very fine whisky which through very healthy sales during that period had every right to be dubbed 'The Centre of Attraction.'

Three years earlier Browne had drawn the soldier being teased while on duty by a poster of Wright and Greig's famous Roderick Dhu brand. Again the theme is the unattainable, though obviously the people here are a lot happier than the guardsman because they could go and buy a bottle if they wished.

At the time of this poster, whisky from Wright and Greig's new distillery at Dallas Dhu would, at two years old, barely have been ready for their Roderick Dhu brand, though legally it could have been used. No spirit produced in Scotland today can be called Scotch until it reaches three years old, but that law did not come into effect until 1916. Wright and Greig were closely tied with Bulloch, Lade so it is almost certain that the blend would have been given a sound weight with their peaty Caol Ila.

Artist: Tom Browne
Date of registration: 23 April 1901
PRO reference: COPY 1/177 f 305

COWAN'S

This most attractive poster for Cowan's Irish whisky is a vast improvement over the one on page 57, though it was drawn many years earlier. Although the characters are dressed in the same traditional clothing there is a compelling sense of fun coupled with reality. With the glorious Irish coastline so superbly portrayed you cannot help feeling that the artist, Felix De Veck, who did such excellent work for Allman's, thoroughly enjoyed his commission.

The meaning of the painting is open to debate. Most likely these are part-time smugglers out to enjoy the whisky for themselves rather than sell on for a profit. Because of extensive German bombing raids on Belfast during the Second World War most records were lost regarding such companies as Cowan's, so regrettably little is known about them. Now they will be best remembered for endearing pieces of period artwork such as this.

Artist: Felix De Veck
Date of registration: 2 July 1891
PRO reference: COPY 1/ 97 f 237

THEY'VE ALL HAD 'BEGG'S'

It is hard to believe that this picture and the success of the brand is down to a chance visit Queen Victoria made to her near neighbour within days of moving into her Balmoral home in the Scottish Highlands. On hearing that they had arrived at their new home, John Begg had sent an invitation to the Royal family to visit his New Lochnagar distillery barely a mile distant. Looking out of a window he noticed to his astonishment the royal party, including Queen Victoria, Prince Albert and their children, advancing to his door. After showing them around his distillery he allowed them to taste his oldest whisky, which at that time could only have been a 3-year-old as the distillery was built in 1845.

Begg was allowed to re-christen his distillery Royal Lochnagar and eventually built up profit enough to enter the blending world with his own brands. From this poster dating from 1912 you can see, amid the sea of smiling, contented faces, that the Royal warrant has been retained. Although John Begg died in 1880 the company continued independently until 1916 when they became too much of a temptation for DCL.

Artist: William Fry
Date of registration: 2 February 1912
PRO reference: COPY 1/318 f 347

They've all had "BEGG'S"

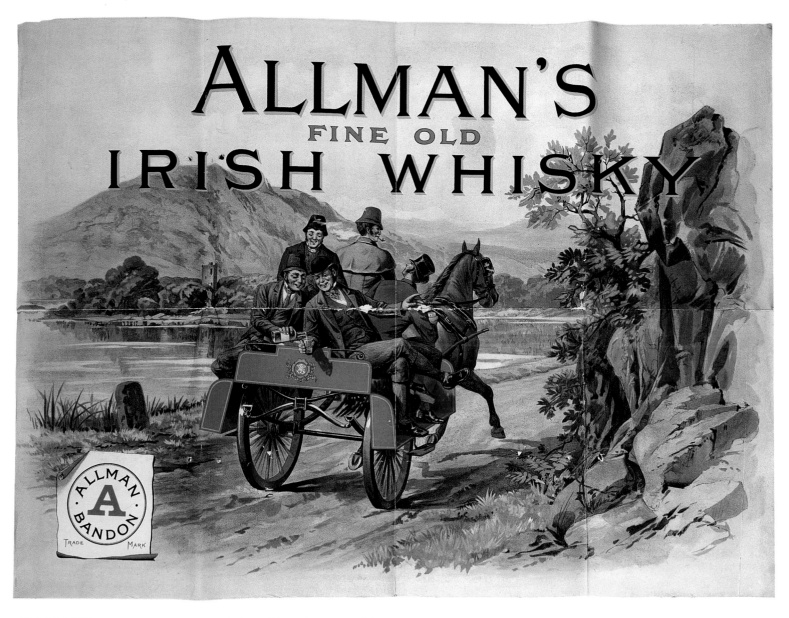

ALLMAN'S

Another well known Irish distiller was James Allman. This stunningly beautiful poster dating all the way back to 1888 perfectly represented the lonely setting of his Bandon distillery. It was nearly 20 miles west of Cork, which in 1826 when he converted a mill into a more profitable enterprise, would have been a very remote location.

When in 1846 his son Richard took over the reins, the company was re-named Allman and Company. By then the distillery had already begun to find markets throughout Ireland. The whiskey made there was the traditional type, a mixture of malted and unmalted barley, but curiously despite its southern location Allman's insisted they made 'whisky' as opposed to 'whiskey'.

At its zenith, perhaps around the time of this poster, some 200 people were employed in an area short of industry and the whiskey was shipped all over the Empire. But following the Irish War of Independence and the secession that followed, the UK market which had ensured the rise of the distillery was cut off not only to them but all other Irish distillers. Cruelly the other natural market, the USA, was also out of reach because of Prohibition. Like many others the company immediately began to find difficulty selling its whiskey and in 1925 the distillery fell silent for the last time. Theirs was a typically sad case of why the Irish whiskey industry shrank so rapidly.

Artist: Felix De Veck
Date of registration: 9 June 1888
PRO reference: COPY 1/82 f106

GULLIVER'S SCOTCH GRAVY

There is something quite intriguing about this poster of a bagpiper looking slightly the worse for wear having apparently got through six bottles of whisky with himself on the label. The name of the blenders of this whisky is Gulliver, a London-based company. Their address is given as 7 Argyll Street and when I mentioned this to former Bell's blender Ian Grieve he immediately latched onto a possible link with Jimmy Gulliver and his company the Argyll Group whose £2.5 billion offer for the Distillers Company was outbid by rivals Guinness during an acrimonious battle in early 1986. Gulliver, who died in 1997, had a distilling background but the Argyll Group dates back only to the early 1970s.

Just as murky is the origination and meaning of the term Scotch 'gravy.' It is a saying I have heard used in casual conversation, though seldom, and could stem from being a slang way of asking to pass the whisky. Or it might even refer to whisky that is poured over the haggis.

Artist: Arthur Penniall
Date of registration: 27 January 1899
PRO reference: COPY 1/146 i f 49

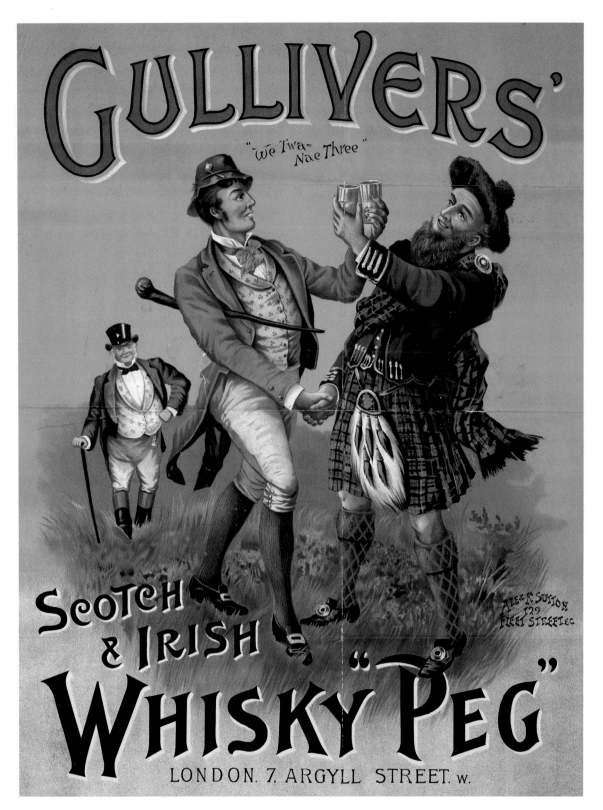

GULLIVERS' WHISKY PEG

It is interesting to note that although this work from the brush of Surrey artist Arthur Penniall was lodged on the same day in 1899 as his 'Scotch Gravy' poster, the lettering for the name Gulliver is slightly different. This suggests that the company had not yet established itself sufficiently to maintain a consistent brand image.

Even so, this is another highly attractive painting and the whisky 'peg' can clearly be seen in the raised hands of the Celtic brethren, the Scotsman and Irishman. A peg was a silver drinking cup and one always associated with another blending firm entirely: 'Take a Peg of John Begg'. These small tankards were perfect for whisky. Originally, though, a peg was also one of a set of pins set inside a drinking vessel which measured the amount each person was allowed to drink. A possible derivation for the word is that it comes from the belief that every time you drink from this vessel, you have just hammered another peg in your coffin.

Artist: Arthur Penniall
Date of registration: 27 January 1899
PRO reference: COPY 1/146 i f 50

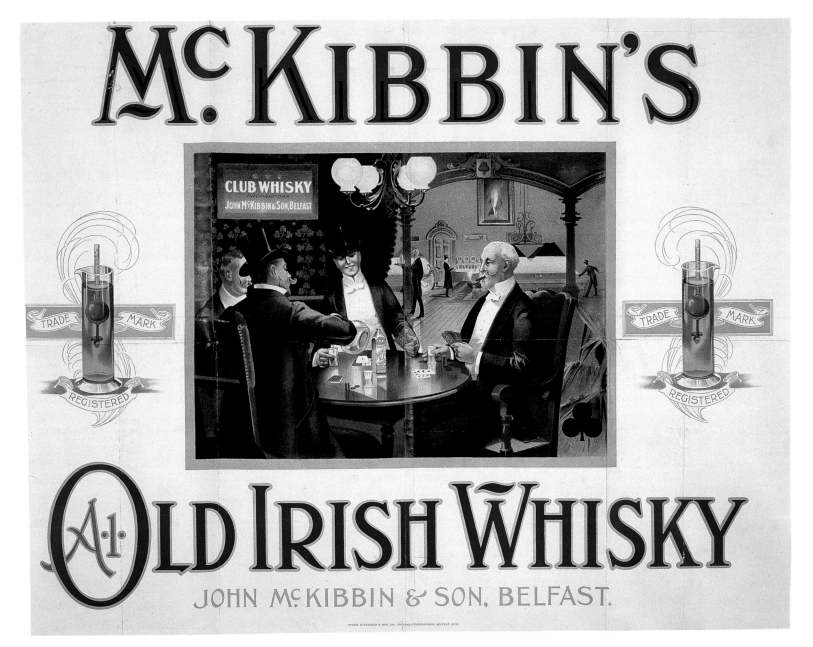

MCKIBBIN'S OLD IRISH WHISKY

McKibbin's were just one of a number of Belfast blenders fighting for their corner of the whisky market using locally produced Irish. From the tone of this poster it appears they were looking to impress wealthier clients. Here we have the epitome of a turn-of-the-century Gentlemen's Club where after a hard day's business men of substance could relax with their peers without a woman or child in sight. This feeling of exclusivity meant the name Club was popular amongst blenders and distillers on both sides of the Atlantic. The most famous of all, Canadian Club, was named as such only because Kentucky bourbon distillers insisted the term Canadian be included so 'Club' whisky from north of the border would not be confused with their own. It was not one of their better decisions.

What is of particular interest to the whisky enthusiast here is not so much the painting of the four men, or the name of the blender, but the highly unusual Trade Mark. The piece of apparatus half submerged in the glass beaker is a perfect representation of the Sikes's hydrometer, the standard piece of equipment used at that time in the distilling trade for the testing of the alcoholic strength of spirit. From the colour of the liquid it is measuring here, this is fully matured whisky.

Artist: Samuel Leighton
Date of registration: 9 June 1900
PRO reference: COPY 1/ 167 f 361

UAM VAR

This blend with the Gaelic name has taken a most un-Gaelic approach to advertising its whisky. Taking into account that the brand name means 'distilled in a cave', here was a chance to continue a rugged Highland theme. Instead it has taken the more dashing, military route favoured by so many companies of the day. And once more it is the lancer who is held up as the benchmark of finesse. The printers, incidentally, are not the Forman company of *Nottingham Evening Post* fame, but the printers Thomas Forman on Hucknall Road who are still in existence though under a new name.

The blenders Innes and Grieve were never major operators and were absorbed by Drambuie, the liqueur company, in the 1920s when they moved into the Innes and Grieve offices in York Place, Edinburgh. Subsequently, Uam Var was made in tiny amounts measured in hundreds rather than thousands of cases and sold only at Cockburns, Edinburgh, until the early to mid 1980s when the brand died out altogether. Drambuie, however, remains a world favourite, a brand first commercially produced by James Ross at the famous Broadford Hotel, Isle of Skye in 1893 after a member of Bonnie Prince Charlie's bodyguard presented the recipe to friends of his family over a century before.

Artist: James Johnstone
Date of registration: 16 July 1907
PRO reference: COPY 1 /260 f 377

CLAN CASTLE

It appears that usually the only people who knew how to spell Sikes's were found at the distilleries and vatting and blending laboratories. 'Sykes's' hydrometer, invented by Bartholomew Sikes, was used as the standard alcohol-measuring equipment from the Hydrometer Act of 1818 right through to 1980 when a new system was adopted where, falling in line with fellow European Community countries, the measurement was given in alcohol by volume. Until 1980 blenders worked to the time-honoured tradition of working out the strength of their whisky by multiplying the reading from their Sikes's hydrometer by .5708. So proof equalled 100 x .5708 which was close on 57.1% alcohol by volume. Whisky was filled into barrel at 11 over proof, which equated to 63.36% alcohol by volume. Here, the bottle says the whisky is 18 under proof. That means the whisky was 47.4% alcohol by volume. In America, bourbon is still given as proof. But there the proof given is exactly twice the alcoholic strength of the whiskey. So 80 proof whiskey is 40% alcohol by volume.

The Clan Castle brand was a popular one promoted by Gilbey's at a time when they still had not used any grain whisky to produce a blend. From the artwork on the bottom of the bottle this appears to be a vatting of their two Speyside distilleries, Glen Spey and Strathmill, of which the latter was the prettier of the two and made the more attractive pure malt.

Artist: Albert Simpson
Date of registration: 2 November 1903
PRO reference: COPY 1/ 209 f 412

WHYTE AND MACKAY

Scotch whisky distillers and blenders were not content with just selling their wares to a grateful British public. As soon as a company became established at home it was customary to set up agents all over the world. Whyte and Mackay were particularly active as exporters and commissioned this calendar specially to cater for customers in New Zealand, with a Maori boy and meeting-house teamed up with a giant bottle of their famous old brand.

The term 'Selected Highland Whisky' was used despite the fact the whisky would have been a blend. The label hardly changed at all until the early 1990s: it still remained easily recognisable as the whisky we see here but this design was finally discarded altogether during a major revamp in 1998.

Whyte and Mackay, though part of the American Jim Beam Brands, have remained an integral part of Glaswegian culture since 1882 when James Whyte and Charles Mackay formed a business partnership as whisky merchants. They called their blend Whyte and Mackay Special, a name which has stuck to this day and ranks in the top half dozen most popular Scotch whiskies. Another impressive link with the past is their method of blending, a long and expensive process of marrying the malts and grains separately and then mixing them together for a second and final marrying process. Most distillers simply add the grains and malts together from the start.

Artist: Edward Hiscocks, of Palmerston North, New Zealand
Date of registration: 20 July 1908
PRO reference: COPY 1/315i f 96

FITZGERALD & CO

This, perhaps the most remarkable of all the designs used to promote whisky in this book, is also one of the most memorable. There is no clichéd nationalism here: just an image which would not look out of place in the most masterful of surreal (yet nationalistic) German films, *The Adventures of Baron Munchausen*. It is a shame, almost, that the poster is promoting one particular brand. The drawing of the bottle then takes on a specific quality that is out of character with the soft tones of the artist's water colour.

In some ways this image of Irish whiskey is also one of the saddest. At the time of its creation the Irish whiskey industry was entering a period of almost irreversible decline. In Dublin such powerful and legendary 'Bank of England' distilleries such as Marrowbone Road, home of William Jameson, and Roe's Thomas Street distillery were to fall to the appalling series of catastrophes which was to hit this industry from 1916 onwards and not make it even into the 1930s. In a sense this poster depicts a once magnificent industry on the wane.

Artist: William Stewart
Date of registration: 6 April 1911
PRO reference: COPY 1/ 306 f 348

SAUNDERS' HOUSE OF LORDS WHISKY

The House of Lords, regarded so often as the last bastion of many of Britain's traditions, obviously believed in the pedigree of Scotch whisky at the turn of the century. That is perhaps why the House of Lords brand stood against the tide by remaining a malt whisky rather than becoming a new-fangled blend.

Despite such auspicious custom and their majestic poster, the Saunders company hardly rose above the ranks of the also rans in the battle for market supremacy. Little is known about them and though at the time the caterer for the House of Commons was a Mr. Saunders, it is hard to believe he was related to this firm as the Government Committee took a dim view of a company's making financial use of the House of Commons' or Lords' name. Indeed even James Buchanan found in 1893 that his whisky orders had been stopped because he had been using the House of Commons as an advertising platform. His whisky was eventually reinstated but only after he had brought the matter to the attention of a friendly Member of Parliament.

There is still a House of Lords whisky, a blend produced by Campbell Distillers, which can be found only in that place plus a few small markets overseas. The brand was launched between the world wars by William Whiteley of Leith, presumably after the Saunders version had failed.

Artist: Edward Smith
Date of registration: 14 October 1905
PRO reference: COPY 1/ 234 f 333

USHER'S WHISKY

And so we end where, in a way, it all began, with Andrew Usher and his Old Vatted Glenlivet brand, probably the very first blended whisky of them all. He is credited with being the first whisky merchant to set out to create the perfect dram by mixing malt whisky with much lighter patent grain whisky, though Charles Mackinlay was very much a close contemporary.

His father, Andrew Usher senior, had set up an Edinburgh-based whisky and spirit business in 1813 so his grounding in the whisky industry could not have been better. But it was only with the relaxation of complex laws regarding the blending of bonded whisky for the home market that merchants could seriously experiment with how the public would react to this very much gentler dram. The results were extraordinary and soon Scotch

whisky became not only a nation's but a world's favourite spirit. The Usher brand continues to this day, only now under the control of UDV as Ushers became part of DCL in 1919.

Trail-blazing blender Andrew Usher died in 1898, six years before this gloriously simple poster was commissioned, having like many other whisky barons contributed to society philanthropically – in his case building the Usher Hall in

Edinburgh. And in many ways this is the proudest poster of them all. The attention is brought only to the bottle, and through the guarantee of quality, what is inside it. So enticing is it, I end this book with a glass of whisky beside me. A nip of Usher's, of course.

Artists: Edward Ellerton, Thomas Rew, Francis Smith and Albert Simpson
Date of registration: 25 March 1904
PRO reference: COPY 1/ 214 f 199

BIBLIOGRAPHY

Andrew, Allen *The Whisky Barons* (Jupiter 1977)

Barnard, Alfred *The Whisky Distilleries of the United Kingdom* (Harper's 1887)

Chisnall, Edward *The Spirit of Glasgow* (Good Books, no date)

Craig, H Charles *The Scotch Whisky Industry Record* (Index Publishing 1994)

Dewar's Ltd *The House of Dewar 1846-1946*

Dewar, Thomas R *A Ramble Round The Globe* (Chatto and Windus 1904)

Gardiner, Leslie *The NB: The First Hundred Years* (North British Distillery 1985)

House, Jack *Pride of Perth* (Hutchinson 1976)

Jameson J, Jameson W, Power J and Roe G, *Truths About Whisky* (London 1878)

Jones, Michael *Time, Gentlemen, Please!* (PRO Publications 1997)

McGuire, E B *Irish Whiskey* (Gill and MacMillan 1973)

Maxwell, Herbert *Half-A-Century of Successful Trade* (Pantheon Press 1907)

Morrice, Philip *The Schweppes Guide to Scotch* (Alphabooks 1983)

Moss, Michael S and Hulme John R *The Making of Scotch Whisky* (James & James 1981)

Murray, Jim *Classic Blended Scotch* (Prion 1998)

Murray, Jim *Classic Irish Whiskey* (Prion 1997)

Murray, Jim *Complete Guide to Whisky* (Carlton 1997)

Murray, Jim *Jim Murray's Complete Book of Whisky* (Carlton 1997)

Murray, Jim *Jim Murray's Irish Whiskey Almanac* (Neil Wilson Publishing 1994)

Nettleton, J A *Manufacture of Whisky and Plain Spirit* (Cornwall & Sons 1913)

Smith, G D *A Book of Words. Whisky* (Carcanet 1993)

Spiller, Brian *The Chameleon's Eye* (James Buchanan & Co 1984)

Weir, Ronald *The History of the Distillers Company, 1877-1939* (Oxford 1995)

Wilson, Ross *The House of Sanderson* (Wm. Sanderson 1963)

Wilson, Ross *Scotch The Formative Years* (Constable 1970)